Storytelling

Master the Art of Telling a Great Story for Purposes of Public Speaking, Social Media Branding, Building Trust, and Marketing Your Personal Brand

© Copyright 2020

All Rights Reserved. No part of this book may be reproduced in any form without permission in writing from the author. Reviewers may quote brief passages in reviews.

Disclaimer: No part of this publication may be reproduced or transmitted in any form or by any means, mechanical or electronic, including photocopying or recording, or by any information storage and retrieval system, or transmitted by email without permission in writing from the publisher.

While all attempts have been made to verify the information provided in this publication, neither the author nor the publisher assumes any responsibility for errors, omissions or contrary interpretations of the subject matter herein.

This book is for entertainment purposes only. The views expressed are those of the author alone, and should not be taken as expert instruction or commands. The reader is responsible for his or her own actions.

Adherence to all applicable laws and regulations, including international, federal, state and local laws governing professional licensing, business practices, advertising and all other aspects of doing business in the US, Canada, UK or any other jurisdiction is the sole responsibility of the purchaser or reader.

Neither the author nor the publisher assumes any responsibility or liability whatsoever on the behalf of the purchaser or reader of these materials. Any perceived slight of any individual or organization is purely unintentional.

Contents

INTRODUCTION 1
CHAPTER 1: WHAT IS STORYTELLING? 2
    TYPES OF STORYTELLING 3
    THE USES OF STORYTELLING 7
CHAPTER 2: THE POWER AND SCIENCE BEHIND STORIES 11
    YOUR BRAIN ON STORYTELLING 12
    EFFECTIVE STORYTELLING THROUGH SCIENCE 13
    STORYTELLING ALONGSIDE SCIENCE 14
    USING MARKETING DATA TO PERPETUATE STORIES AND CHANGES IN YOUR LIFE 18
CHAPTER 3: FINDING YOUR STORY 20
    ACTIVITY 21
    STILL STUCK? DO THESE ACTIVITIES 25
    THE TEST OF FINDING YOUR STORY – IS IT MEANINGFUL? 26
CHAPTER 4: CRAFTING YOUR STORY 28
    CRAFTING CHECKLIST 28
    SPECIAL NOTES ON VISUAL ELEMENTS OF STORY CRAFTING 40
CHAPTER 5: FIVE ELEMENTS OF A GOOD STORY 41
    ACTIVITY 47

CHAPTER 6: STORYTELLING IN PUBLIC SPEAKING 53
How Is Public Speaking Different? 54
CHAPTER 7: STORYSELLING: STORYTELLING AS A MARKETING TOOL 60
What is Storyselling? 61
Consumers Want Storyselling 62
How and Where to Deliver Stories to Consumers 63
Resources for Storyselling 65
Special Notes for Marketers 67
CHAPTER 8: SOCIAL MEDIA AND INFLUENCER STORYTELLING 68
What the Pros on Digital Marketing Say About Influencers 68
Influencer and Social Media Marketing are the Future - Tips for Using These Tools 70
Practical Tips for Influencer Marketing with Storytelling 72
CHAPTER 9: DIGITAL STORYTELLING 75
Is It Storytelling, Digital Storytelling, or Something Else? 76
Let's Talk Platform 78
Digital Storytelling Examples 79
How Can You Start a Digital Story? 80
Best Practices for Digital Storytelling 81
Tools to Use in Digital Storytelling 84
CHAPTER 10: IMMERSIVE STORYTELLING 85
Immersive Storytelling Through History 86
Where to Start and Outlining Tips 87
Platforms for Immersive Storytelling 91
Tools for Building Immersive Stories 93
CHAPTER 11: 7 EXPERTS ON STORYTELLING 95
CHAPTER 12: THE FUTURE OF STORYTELLING 103
CONCLUSION 108
RESOURCES 109

Introduction

How often do you use stories in your life? Storytelling is an integral part of everyone's life, whether they know it or not. This comprehensive guide can take you from being a beginning storyteller to a pro with tangible information and actionable tips. Spring into your storytelling by learning how to find your story, and then deliver it compellingly with expert insight.

This book will help you develop a deep understanding of the latest trends so that you can adapt your stories to suit your audience after learning the basics of storytelling. Use the tools here to begin implementing storytelling into your role as a business professional, speaker, parent, teacher, and much more. The art and craft of storytelling is a talent you can apply in nearly every area of life.

It does not matter if you have any experience in storytelling; you can get started while learning the fundamentals and gain valuable tools in the process.

Chapter 1: What is Storytelling?

Storytelling goes far beyond what most people expect. It is not only a way to convey a series of events; it also evokes emotion. With a simple story, you can convince someone to question their morals, change their ethical values, and even alter the course of their life. Few other methods of communication can spur as much emotional and behavioral responses as storytelling. That is precisely why so many people are turning to storytelling for marketing, branding, teaching, and even parenting.

Now, not all storytelling is made equal, and this book will soon get into the different types of storytelling. First, storytelling needs to be defined from a birds-eye perspective clearly.

The standard definition of storytelling is the act of crafting or creating a story. However, that definition does not specify whether the story has to be real or fictional or how the story is conveyed. As you read through this book, you will see that the art of storytelling can apply to business professionals, marketers, Church officials, parents, teachers, and others, because all storytelling has a single goal.

The purpose of storytelling is to deliver some cultural history and personal identity to the audience. In recent years, the role of storytelling has emerged dramatically across multiple media outlets and platforms. It seems that although storytelling has been around since the dawn of man, there has been a recent shift in how and where stories are shared.

Storytelling delivers facts or information through a narrative that is relatable and has an impact.

Types of Storytelling

Not every story is the same, but not every story is unique, either. In fiction, you have a few familiar stories, such as the hero/epic tale, the journey-driven tale of growth, or the coming-of-age novel. In storytelling, through the use of marketing, teaching, parenting, and leading, there are five primary types of stories.

These five types are not so exclusive that you can't step outside of these bubbles. However, you will be pretty surprised to find that most of your stories fit into at least one of these molds.

1. "Who am I?" Story

It gives an introduction to a character/s, including backstories, life purposes, and more. You can unintentionally do this with business titles or a defensive approach. When misused, these stories can quickly go wrong.

However, the humbler and more human these stories are, the more effective they become. What is important to remember with the *Who am I?* story is not to depict the best possible version of yourself. There is a difference between:

"I started life in a small country town, one of those little fly-by states, and now I'm a CMO of a Fortune 500 company. I drive my dream car and take vacations to Italy at least once a year."

And

"You probably wouldn't know the town I'm from if I told you the name. It's a small town, and I learned a lot there while growing up. I should probably take more vacations home, but I have these opportunities now that I just can't pass up. Those opportunities only came to me because of where I started life, where I'm from, and ..."

When writing a *Who am I?* story remember that you are not your job or your material possessions, or your most significant accomplishments. Storytelling calls for that underlayer, that private part of your life to come to the surface.

2. "Why am I Here?" Story

It gives a sense of connection when people are clear regarding their goals and purpose in being present. The *Why am I here?* story is most common in conferences, business settings, and interviews. However, teachers frequently use this story when speaking with the parents of their students. The key to a *Why am I here?* story is transparency. If you are there to make a sale or convince someone, tell them. Here are two examples, one is far more effective than the other:

"Everyone here at this conference today has come together for a common goal. Together we can make changes in energy conservation and change energy consumption. Energy can manage exactly that, and it's ready to go within the next 24 months."

Or

"Experts show us that increased energy consumption is inevitable, which means that focusing on energy conservation and lowering consumption is a losing battle. Except, I'm here to put energy use into a different light. I want all of you here to consider a new way of thinking about energy consumption."

The *Why am I here?* story serves a particular purpose in explaining the connection between the storyteller and the audience. Often you will hear these types of stories in TEDx Talks, at conferences, and in well-covered news stories. In fact, the opening line, "We're standing here today on..." is present in most on-scene news coverage stories because of the precision this story structure lends.

3. Visionary

These stories come into play when there is a goal that seems unattainable, and you need those people to envision the reality you see. Most prolific examples of this include the *I Have a Dream* speech from Martin Luther King Jr. The *I Have a Dream* speech painted a picture of a genuine possibility and gave clear conditions and expectations at the end.

Visionary stories must be used sparingly to protect their role in storytelling. If everyone told visionary stories all the time, what is now a tool to sway people toward a desirable future would become raw fiction. You can undoubtedly look at famous works of fiction and see the visionary narrative in hindsight, but these tales are best told with a present tense goal.

The *I Have a Dream* speech clearly shows how successful King was as a prolific speaker because of his storytelling abilities. He spoke of past events in present speak, as in this example:

"Five score years ago a great American... This momentous decree is a great beacon of hope to millions..."

And then, he brings the past and current struggles and marries them with the visionary future here:

"I have a dream that one day... a state sweltering with the heat of injustice... will be transformed into an oasis of freedom and justice."

Now, it is hard to follow Dr. King. However, it's clear here that there are specific words and conceptual requirements necessary for a compelling visionary tale. When deciding if you have a visionary story to share, look for:

- Past strife, struggle, or missed opportunities
- Use the phrase "will be"
- Speech patterns that suggest there is a clear divide between the past, present, and future.

4. Educational Story

A critical type of story, but usually not the opening in a lecture, speech, or any other forum. Educational stories must exist not only to inform but convince. Without the convincing element, an educational story is just a list of facts or possible insights. The story is the vessel for delivering information. They must work together.

One example could be selling the business model of Uber. Can you imagine the pitch? You would not show up and say, "Hey, let's allow strangers to drive people around for less money than a cab." However, you might give an educational story like this:

"Uber is perfect for a pub crawl without a DD." Or "It's the alternative to spending hundreds on a rental car."

These stories can be short or long, but they need to depict the information while remaining engaging clearly.

5. "I Know What You're Thinking..." - Branding Story

Although you need to really hone these stories before you move forward, this is the last attempt to convert people. Often these stories appear in branding, and you must understand precisely where your previous stories went wrong with this group. Not every story will hit home with everyone, and the *I know what you're thinking* approach allows for the acceptance of the skeptics.

Parents are pros at this story even though it's not technically branding. They are the ones put into the spotlight of adopting and adapting different perspectives that are difficult to understand.

You have probably heard, "I know it's hard right now, but it gets easier later." Which is the foundation or one-sentence reference to this story's purpose. A more in-depth storytelling version might be:

"I know our expectations seem high right now. When my sister was a teenager, she failed almost every class, and every year we thought she was going to get held back. That didn't change, but eventually, she graduated. Then, she decided she wanted to own a salon instead of working for one. That meant she needed to learn how to open and run a business, which she eventually learned. She went to a local college, nothing fancy, but she did well. It was the first time she excelled in school, and now she wishes she hadn't waited so long. I know you think that school isn't necessary right now, but no matter what, learning is vital for your future."

The Uses of Storytelling

Storytelling has many uses, and often people use storytelling without consciously choosing to. From parenting to business professionals and everything in between, storytelling can serve a significant purpose. An individual can share an experience, give a cautionary tale, inform others, and prove a point.

You may not realize it, but you might already use storytelling as an integral part of your life. People use storytelling at work to teach and connect with colleagues. Friends use storytelling to build relationships and gain new perspectives. Parents and teachers use storytelling to give content and simplify complex matters for children.

Branding and Marketing

What possible role could storytelling have in marketing and advertisements (ads)? Some of your favorite stores and brands probably use storytelling. They use it to connect with their customers and show the world their values as a brand. Company values and being transparent about them can drastically impact a business's market position.

To use storytelling in marketing and branding, companies may create a character or give a narrative that puts the consumer as the main character.

To introduce storytelling into a brand or marketing campaign, you need to consider the technical elements:

- Will you create a character? (Martin the Geico Gecko, Flo of Progressive, the Aflac Duck)

- Is your story one ongoing narrative? (Nike Just Do It, Hinge)
- Will your story progress and change? (Taco Bell Movie commercials, Johnsonville "sausage" commercials)
- How will your character or narrative directly relate to the brand's ideal audience?

o Aflac Duck is extremely accident prone.

o Nike's commercials showrunners and other athletes in their ideal environment.

o Airbnb focuses on the people – the homeowners and the people booking.

o Huggies – shows the joys and struggles of parenting.

o Warby Parker – uses images to identify with glasses wearers and delivers on their promise of designer eyewear at bargain prices.

Hinge is a great example, not only because they are somewhat new to breaking into mass marketing but also because of their approach.

Hinge markets themselves to the "singletons who are over the game," which essentially calls out Tinder and other swiping apps. That is not a discrete attempt at a rivalry. In fact, it is very Coke vs. Pepsi of them. The rivalry is the backstory of every Hinge user. It begs the question, "Are you tired of hookups, awkward encounters, and people looking to play the field?" They back that up with hard facts to support their side of the Hinge vs. hookup app campaign.

So how does Hinge tell their story?

Hinge shows a furry app monster, appearing in a variety of situations that normal couples or dating people face. But the real "main character" is the user. It dares its users to explore "The app that's meant to be deleted" because you should find true love and a fulfilling relationship. They solidify that by destroying/killing off the monster in nearly every ad. It is a recurring story that changes but does not progress. It's a Dating Apocalypse.

The primary message from the Hinge is its core brand purpose. They even go so far as to establish "out-of-home" ads in the form of billboards. A stark contrast to what you expect from modern-day dating apps. Even so, those billboards tell second-person narratives of dates, showing an ideal ending to a date that would lead to a long-term relationship.

SoulCycle, another great example, has used such powerful storytelling in its branding that it is borderline becoming a cult. In fact, the storytelling is so good that people will pay the price of a monthly gym membership for a single class. They offer a top-of-the-line fitness experience that challenges the traditional gym atmosphere.

SoulCycle uses storytelling by showing the "SOUL experience." Where Hinge used commercials, SoulCycle relies on platforms such as Instagram, its website, and other media outlets. On their Instagram, they urge people to "Join the movement." Then it shows a near endless stream of happy and empowered people anticipating their next SoulCycle class. They sprinkle in some self-care and personal wellness plans for an extra dose of trust building.

Teachers and Speakers

Outside of branding and marketing, teachers and speakers employ storytelling the most. Teachers present stories, physically, to their classes daily. Speakers can range from a legal representative to someone who addresses the team before a shift starts. These "in-person" storytellers must be consciously aware of not only their story and the narrative but also their physical presence. Tim Cook, who speaks at the Apple conference each year, is one example of a speaker with excellent storytelling skills and is very aware of his physical presence. TEDx Talks usually have speakers who are also very aware of their physical presence.

Teachers, business professionals, and other forms of speakers approach storytelling with a more concept-oriented purpose than branding and marketing. Where advertising is clearly meant to sell, teachers and speakers are providing information, urging people to challenge their thinking and more.

Storytelling has a massive part in promoting development, enabling people to adopt new perspectives, and getting people to "buy-in." There is never a point at which teachers stop using storytelling. There is never a point where business professionals can consistently build business relationships and develop their staff without using storytelling somehow.

Others who use storytelling regularly include:

- Public officials
- Copywriters, authors, and bloggers
- Company speakers or representatives (legal counsel, department heads, press reps)
- School administrators and officials
- Church speakers
- Parents

Every industry employs storytelling, and its power in engagement and captivation is undeniable. With proper storytelling, you can better yourself, build your business, and much more. However, storytelling is not just recounting fables and old wives' tales. Instead, it is a scientifically proven method for effective communication and impactful marketing.

Chapter 2: The Power and Science Behind Stories

Storytelling has long been the best way to move people. It might not be the most efficient, but it is the most effective. Why? The whole point of storytelling is to connect with an audience and share an experience. Through storytelling, you can accomplish emotional connection and behavioral change that raw facts simply cannot achieve.

Now, when you break down the science of storytelling, what you are looking at is the human response to emotional engagement. As the storyteller, you can prompt different hormones, such as dopamine and endorphins.

Without a doubt, Aesop, Homer, and the tribal leaders who shared oral tales of legend and caution were not thinking about the brain's reaction to storytelling. That didn't make the stories or lessons any less valid. However, with a bit of knowledge about the science behind storytelling, you can drastically impact your story to make it more effective, memorable, and applicable to your audience. The science behind storytelling spans across a broad reach from the craft and structure to the response you seek from the listeners. This book will cover the foundational principles and significant findings from the scientific community.

Your Brain on Storytelling

You may recall the "this is your brain on (insert drug or substance here)" commercials. Your brain is arguably the most vital organ in your body because, without it, all other functions cease almost immediately. Your mind is the control center, but when listening to a story, you are giving someone else access to some of the controls.

Through storytelling, your brain will listen, and then, in a stroke of genius in biological creation, your mind imagines you in that position. This superpower is one reason why so many people enjoy historical accounts, fantasy and science-fiction, and other fictional storytelling. However, your brain is just as adept at imagining new or far off places as it is at reimagining you as the main character in a rather dull story.

"You're never going to kill storytelling because it's built into the human plan. We come with it." - Margaret Atwood, author of *The Handmaid's Tale*.

As Margaret Atwood put it, humans simply come with the ability to tell stories and take them into themselves. Science backs that up with support from recent studies that show that more centers of the brain light up and work collaboratively when listening to a story. There is a systematic chain reaction that literally resembles the depth and dedication a person has when connecting to a story.

First, you get the line, and your language processing center initiates the intake of the verbal information. Second, in your language comprehension, a different part of the brain kicks in. Now, that part of the brain is putting the language into a usable context. It is not changing the story; it's making it relatable. That part of your brain might associate a feeling of sadness with the completely unrelated experience to spur the emotion described in the story. After the language comprehension center becomes active, your memory centers activate. Those memory centers feed the language comprehension center in a give and take patter. Imagine that your language centers are sitting around with your hippocampus, cerebellum, and prefrontal cortex having a "remember when" conversation. That communication will prompt another part of the brain, the hypothalamus, to get to work. It releases and creates hormones, communicates with the nervous system, and more.

The response of your brain when listening to a story is almost the same as if you were experiencing the events yourself.

As your brain processes the information and stirs up past emotion, you begin to notice the physical responses. When listening to a thrilling story, your brain will tell your adrenal gland to turn on and produce cortisol. That cortisol goes right back to the brain and says, "We're in distress! There are potential threats!" It can make it uncomfortable to sit still as your heart rate increases, and you experience a cold sweat or goosebumps.

Or, if the story is a happy one, the hypothalamus will produce dopamine, or any other "feel good" hormones. You will become relaxed or enticed. You may lean forward, uncross your arms or legs, and rest your chin on your hands. You are enthralled, but not scared.

Modern research has confirmed what elders have known for centuries. Stories make people feel something more significant than what they usually experience as they provoke a response that other triggers just can't create.

Effective Storytelling through Science

People now know, without a doubt, what a compelling story can do to one's brain. So how can you take that information and create your own effective story? It is actually somewhat formulaic.

Aim to achieve:

1. *Emotional response* - Putting the reader in the shoes of the primary character/teller.

2. *Give an issue an identity* - Emphasize the importance of the problem and possible impact or consequences.

3. *Connect a greater audience to a specific challenge* - evoke a connection through shared human experience.

4. *Make the audience feel humanized* - avoid dramatizing events past the emotional scope of the bulk of society, but also trust that your readers will understand the story.

5. *Raise the stakes* - give your story a do or die moment.

6. *Show the effects rather than tell* - evocation of emotion through visual cues.

You do not need to try and reach the entire human population. You need to reach your audience with these six goals that scientifically mark compelling storytelling.

It will take time to develop each of these in your story, and primarily you will notice them through the editing process. After you find your story and commit it to paper, you have the opportunity to thoroughly evaluate what you have created for each of these elements. Do not overwhelm yourself by trying to implement all of these goals at once. Some may occur naturally in your story and others you may need to create by altering the language, changing the pacing, or giving more (or less) information.

Storytelling Alongside Science

Nat Kendall-Taylor is one speaker who works in the field of psychological anthropology. He shared in a viral TEDx Talk about the commonalities of human experience and cultural engagement. When working on your story, consider with high regard the likelihood that many other humans have opinions and experiences with hot topic issues that might seem too big for comprehension.

Through shared cultural development and the human ability to empathize with someone, people have changed how they think and make decisions. That human experience and cultural engagement can help storytellers and the audience. Consider that someone who has never experienced food scarcity or racial inequality will still have a response because of cultural experience, and often, those developed responses are very predictable.

One of the ways to govern that predictable response is to sprinkle your story with factual basis and scientific research. Using science in a story keeps the relevance on the intended impact. However, when you combine expert opinion and scientific research while pairing that with public opinion, you have a culture. That is the ideal situation for a powerful story.

Facts alone will not achieve the desired results, no matter how much it should create a predictable outcome. A story alone may accomplish those results, but for impact and efficacy, combine the two with an emphasis on culture, minor parts in facts, and acknowledging the public opinion.

You can use those shared cultural experiences, alongside fact, to achieve the six goals discussed earlier.

What you are doing at this point is marrying science, culture, human experience, and your story. You do this by doing the thing that was discussed earlier in this chapter—provoking hormone creation. It is a full-circle event, and you do not have to start anywhere in particular.

Within good storytelling, the human mind is likely to experience:

- Vasopressin
- Serotonin
- Dopamine
- Endorphins
- Oxytocin
- Endorphins

Perhaps the most important are dopamine, oxytocin, and endorphins. The presence of dopamine results in increased focus, better memory building, and a boost in motivation. It makes you want to get out and do something, something meaningful, and you will remember why.

Oxytocin promotes generosity, trust, and bonding, which means that it makes people feel more human. It heightens the human qualities that everyone experiences together, and so it is a shared human experience. Generating oxytocin has a built-in double-down effect. Because the story itself is prompting oxytocin and making you feel connected, when the oxytocin kicks in, you are really committed and engaged.

Finally, endorphins make you feel good. They make you relaxed and at ease.

However, when an audience begins to experience cortisol and adrenaline, they worry. The audience experiences anxiety, an increased heart rate, and an unsettled feeling. These two hormones, primarily when they are together, make people feel:

- Uncreative
- Irritable
- Critical

That is the effect of most storytelling in the workplace and even through marketing. All too often, storytellers want to create a sense of urgency, and they believe that to do that, they need to shock the listener or audience and make them feel like they need to move *now*. You will get much better results of building anticipation, motivation, and then getting a meaningful outcome if you focus more on creating that first list of hormones.

There is a bit of a cheat sheet when it comes to creating hormones, particularly within storytelling:

- To create endorphins, make your audience laugh.
- To create dopamine, you use cliffhangers and then deliver on those cliffhangers.

- To create oxytocin, you create empathy by establishing transparency and authenticity.
- To create all three, focus on building suspense.

Then to implement those, use these three tips:

1. Understand that there is no "right" narrator; you are your narrator.

2. Write out your stories and dissect them for the actions/reactions listed above.

3. Index those stories based on hormone association to build a sturdy "good-feeling" or "impactful" story.

Now, there is a vast market that is already doing this: marketers and advertising teams. For decades now, companies have created stories meant to spur those hormones, to create the desired response, and they have done so with substantial success.

For example, Luvs, a famous diaper brand that often falls third in line behind Huggies and Pampers, uses storytelling. They accept and even identify that they are not Pampers and Huggies because their story is that parents choose Luvs with their second child.

Paint a picture of one commercial: Two parents struggle over a tiny baby bath device, while the newborn cries, and are fighting over general cleaning practices. Then (years later), the hurried mom runs to the back bedroom with a partially naked child and sees the dad in the shower. They do a well-honed hand-off, and it is clear that they've been successful at this parenting bit for a while now. Then it shows the mom taking an older and already clean child in to get ready for bed. The commercial narrator says, "By their second kid, every parent is an expert and more likely to choose Luvs than first-time parents." After that mention, it shows an absorbency comparison against a Huggies diaper.

That commercial is a perfect example of storytelling confirmed through science. They offer a story that nearly all parents can identify: the struggle and stress of bathing a newborn while being completely inexperienced. Then, it shows the success model and makes the viewers laugh, that "Here's your kid, clean it up" moment during the hand-off. Finally, it offers a stat, which Luvs identified through their studies—that most Luvs users have a second child or more. It seals the deal with absorbency. It gave culture, public perception, facts, and displayed scientific insight for the viewer to experience.

Using Marketing Data to Perpetuate Stories and Changes in Your Life

"Marketing is no longer about the stuff you buy, but the stories you tell." - Seth Godin

Although there have been professional storytellers outside of entertainment for decades now, the proof is finally coming out. Because of storytelling-driven marketing and the data that marketing teams capture, you can set precise numbers to how convincing and impactful a story is.

Harrington Communications published a study where 80 percent of people remembered things that they had viewed or experienced. As stated at the beginning of this chapter, the memorable point is the purpose of achieving this experience or viewership. That experience all comes from ensuring your story is meaningful, useful, and achieves specific goals.

The second step you will look at for storytelling validation comes from the same Harrington Communications study. They found that 75 percent of viewers would go directly to the company's website after watching a branded video that contained a message delivered through storytelling. A little later, this book will detail how multiple mediums come into play during modern storytelling. Where a few decades ago, storytelling was American author, salesman, and motivation speaker Zig Ziglar—sharing his experiences from a stage, with people who were interested and sought out that information—now storytelling is put into multiple platforms and can reach unexpected audiences.

What does that tell you about storytelling? It shows that it has a scientific foundation in changing the way people think and convincing them of something new. While marketing is mostly seen as an artistic department within a business, it is incredibly data-driven.

There is data behind deciding on a color palette or choosing one font over another. Where marketers in prior decades have spent excessive amounts of time choosing color schemes and fonts, marketers are now doing that for storytelling-driven branding. They are pouring over data, and creating even more data about storytelling, making this art much more scientific. When you bring in what modern-day researchers are learning about brain activity during storytelling and listening, it is clear that storytelling is not just art, but science.

Chapter 3: Finding Your Story

Most people struggle to find their stories because they do not believe they have much to tell. You definitely have a story worth telling that will echo with others and have a meaningful impact. Particularly if you are a business owner or entrepreneur, you have experienced something: opening a business that many are interested in but are too afraid actually to do. The story of how you realized your business was your passion, and eventually founding your company, is a tale of passion, risk, and excitement. Everyone has stories that are worth sharing, and this book will help you find yours.

So, where do you start? How can one go about finding their story, and is there more than one to tell? Start by identifying the possible key moments in your life. Even if they seem insignificant or utterly normal to you, it could have been the catalyst for leading you to where you are now. Remember that every story has a beginning, and that beginning does not have to be the date you were born. Often the beginning of a story is one moment that impacted how you thought about the world around you and changed your behaviors.

Activity

Make a short list of the moments in your life that you remember most vividly. Recall what was mentioned in Chapter 2—the use of a memorable point and that every story should start with one. That is where this exercise comes into play. Write down between five and ten memorable points in your life. There is no requirement for a level of interest. They can be dull.

If you are skeptical of this activity as a starting point for finding your story, look at a famous fiction story that started with something very normal for the main character.

The Hobbit by J.R.R. Tolkien began with a brief explanation of hobbits. However, in that brief introduction, Tolkien communicated that Bilbo Baggins was probably the most boring and most typical hobbit anyone, including himself, could imagine. Then he had one very normal (albeit rather frustrating) encounter with Gandalf, which changed Bilbo's life. That one chance encounter of saying hello led from one thing to another and another until he was face to face with the dragon Smaug.

Now, *The Hobbit* is a fictional tale, and clearly, it did not actually happen—at least not in this world. But it is still good storytelling. It starts with that unsuspected memorable and pivotal moment when Bilbo met Gandalf, and Gandalf decided that the hobbit would become a thief.

The key lesson that you can take away from this J.R.R. Tolkien classic is that seemingly insignificant moments lead to life-changing events. That one conversation drastically changed Bilbo's life and altered his identity so radically that he would become excitable and adventurous—the very opposite of the boring hobbit on page one.

While you are building your list of moments in life, think of the possible encounters. So much of people's lives revolve around people and relationships. What moments and meetings in your life have drastically changed who you are as a person? Was it one job interview that went really well, or maybe very poorly? Perhaps it was the day you met your spouse, which changed the course of your life, career, and financial plans.

People's lives and stories are made up of tiny moments that lead to other tiny moments that collectively are massive changes. As you are finding your story, look for these tiny moments, and question their degree of impact. Even if the story you tell is not necessarily about a college experience or job-based story, explore your college interview or first job interview. What were you like? What was the interviewer like? Were you so different all those years ago?

You were probably very young and didn't have the full skill set necessary to thrive without help, but there, across the table, was a person of authority asking you questions that would decide your immediate future.

Approach this as an exercise because what you have on your initial list probably won't end up as the beginning of your first great story. The first story you use for your brand, in a classroom, or day-to-day life, doesn't have to be prolific, but usually, people know what they want to write, and they hesitate until they realize that it is the right story.

Another possibility of finding your story is an incredibly unique story. Some people genuinely do live lives that seem as though they are straight out of fiction. It is why the phrase "You couldn't have made that up if you tried" exists. Often, life really is stranger than fiction. But these events seem so rare and often unfortunate.

There are people out there in the world that now live normal lives, but their past is something more complicated than what most people can imagine. Former cult members, victims of stalking, survivors of murder attempts, and life-threatening disasters, all have stories that perplex and enthrall everyone else.

While many stories do start with a rather ordinary moment in time, others involve critical pivot points. Do not shy away from stories that drag out an unhappy, shocking, or even traumatic past.

One great example is a personal story from Kathleen Baty, better known as The Safety Chick. Now, Kathleen runs a business called The Safety Chick and lives a normal life. If you met her on the street, you would never guess the story she has to tell, but if you follow her brand, you will intimately know her story. Kathleen's story is her brand story. It is the reason that she founded her business and has dedicated her life to helping people enhance their awareness of their surroundings and improve their personal safety skills.

Kathleen Baty was stalked by a former high school classmate for over a decade. After years of stalking, the stalker broke into her home and held her at gunpoint. She notes in her story that at that point, she was prepared for anything to happen mentally, but chance and strategic thinking allowed her to contact emergency services, get a SWAT team on site, and with her hands tied behind her back, she jumped a very typical white picket fence to get to safety. That is the story Kathleen shares when she talks about why she founded The Safety Chick, and it hits people hard. Why are people so impacted by a story that doesn't have any element that they have experienced?

The commonality from this unique experience and Kathleen's audience in most situations is the shared risk. Anyone could be the victim of stalking, and everyone needs to learn personal protection. It is likely that even if you have never been stalked or attacked, you can still understand that dreaded feeling of walking through a dark parking lot alone. It's unsettling, and through using her story to draw attention to her brand and business, Kathleen has helped many people learn defensive techniques and built awareness about stalking victims.

So how do you know if your story contains a critical pivot point? Honestly, you will know. Abuse, trying times, challenges faced in a new job or new location, and family troubles can all be unique critical pivot points. These are the stories that break perceptions or change how people think about the teller and others who have been in their situation.

Circling back to the Kathleen Baty example, her stalking started before the Internet, but social media made it worse. The standard public answer is that if someone is bothering you online, stop signing in. However, with Baty, that wasn't sufficient. That is one major perception break that her audiences almost always experience unless they have previously heard her story.

Now you have a list of memorable moments starting points, or a few critical pivot points. What next?

Ask these questions to start to determine if you've found your story or maybe to work toward what the *real* story is from your starting points.

- Why did this happen? (Remember that not all stories are "your" stories).
- Was the event preventable?
- Was it intentional?
- Does your story inspire you now?

Pull together your answers to these questions and allow yourself to wander. As you wander, you can determine if your particular story has clearly connected points, or if you are uncovering many disconnected, but smaller, stories.

Then you want to determine the motivation for the story and the purpose of telling it. What will this story accomplish, and why should you share it? Answering these questions can only come from exploring the story, trying it out, and then, after maybe a few paragraphs or even a full first draft, determining that it is the right story to tell now, and for the right audience.

Still Stuck? Do These Activities

1. Carry a Notebook

Carrying a notebook can help or use a note-taking app. Apps such as Trello, OneNote, or Evernotes are also useful and can help keep your thoughts in order and easy to see. Make a note whenever you notice that something did matter in your life. Or make a note when you realize that when you're in normal conversation, you revert to the same handful of stories.

2. Record Your Thoughts – Journaling for Reference

Recording your thoughts on an audio note or in a journal is great because you can reference back to that material whenever you're crafting a story in the future. Using modern journaling apps such as Day One is useful for searching with particular words, and cataloging journal entries with pictures. It can make it easy to find your thoughts and feelings that you were reflecting on at that time. However, if you prefer the old pen and paper method, you can use a few tricks to make it easy to reference. If you know that you're reflecting on a few major topics, or even just between sad and happy emotions, use color-coded tabs or highlighters. Then you can quickly flip through the pages and get a sense of what you have on each page.

3. Document Life-Changing Events as they Happen

Life-changing events are almost always happening, but particular times stick out and deserve special attention. Imagine people that journaled what they experienced following the events of 9/11. Could you have journaled what you were doing during the 2008 recession or the COVID-19 shelter-in-place order? Many people keep specific journals for their time just before or just after getting married. Others journal through their time opening a business or when starting a new career.

4. Get to Know Yourself Better

Nothing is as helpful in finding your story than finding yourself. Too often, people get lost in portraying their best selves, and then there's the argument of authenticity. Are you the person you are in front of others or when you're alone? Can you be both? Getting to know yourself better is a long but gratifying process. It not only helps you uncover your stories but understand them better, too.

The Test of Finding Your Story – Is It Meaningful?

If it is not meaningful to you, then it certainly won't be meaningful to anyone else. Your story must be unique, offer insight, and give perspective into your experiences and help others learn more about themselves. However, many people struggle to find their story and then deliver it in an impactful manner. It is easy to say, "Oh, this happened when I was a child," or "Then I got laid off, and things got worse."

Finding your story is not just about identifying the moment where you will eventually start your story. It is about realizing what led up to it and how it was resolved. As the teller, you must know all the backstory and everything that came after. While storytelling certainly differs from writing a novel or short story, it should follow the same basic structure of beginning-middle-end. Thus, you should have rising action, the climax, and the falling action.

Beginning with the beginning, it is tough to know where to start. However, every story has a beginning, and most stories begin *in medias res*. In medias res is a Latin phrase that means to start "in the midst of things." Your audience, whether that is your social media following or an audience physically in front of you, does not need all the backstory to understand your story. They also don't need or want to know everything that came after the resolution. Have some peace of mind while working on finding your story regarding how you don't need to know *exactly* the beginning point, climax, or endpoint, just yet.

As you go from finding your story or maybe experimenting with possible stories, you will need to learn more about crafting them—how to use structure, tone, and pacing to move forward.

Chapter 4: Crafting Your Story

Crafting your story demands that you know exactly what story you are telling. You need to nuance out a few details, such as what happens in the beginning, middle, and end, and how you will get to each point. Unfortunately, learning to craft a story only comes through the act of doing it. As you start to flush out your story and what each segment should accomplish, you'll realize that there are certain functions and processes you have to go through.

To start, here are the fundamentals you need to know your character; your voice is a narrator, the function of the storytelling triangle, and the outline of your plot. After you define these elements of your story, you can dive into the actual writing. However, once you have written out your story, it does not mean that you are done. This book refers to crafting a story rather than writing a story because there are many steps in this process, and it could perpetuate forever. What helps most people in their new storytelling is to have a substantial checklist to refer back to.

Crafting Checklist

- Establish the point of your story
- Clearly define your character or characters

- Limit the scope of your narrator – do they know everything or only their perspective?
- Write your story – Using structure to help guide development
- Review each part of your story for authenticity
- Edit each section for clarity
- Review and edit again for emotional connection
- Review and edit a final time for ease of reading and enjoyment

This list is just something to reference back to as you are crafting your story. You're going to dive deeply into each of these points so that you have a complete guide on how to move forward with writing your first story, editing it, and going through the general crafting process.

Step One: Establish Your Point

"A story is already over before we hear it. That is how the teller knows what it means." – Joan Silber

As mentioned in Chapter 1, there are five primary types of stories. Your first goal before you start outlining, but after you find your story, is to establish your point. Is this a "who am I?" story or an educational story?

Now the point of your story does not always have to be in your audience's face. It can be very subtle. Some of the top storytellers in the world, who excellently established their point without overtly preaching to their audience, work for Pixar.

To see the purpose of establishing a point and the role that this step will play in crafting your story, look no further than Pixar's *Wall-e*.

Wall-e opens with a very positive robot cleaning up a very desolate Earth. Then, during the rising action segment, the audience comes to understand that Wall-e is one of the thousands of robots left with the charge of cleaning up the Earth that humans destroyed.

That is where the point comes into play because Pixar does very well at establishing their point early. Without saying anything, they show Earth in its terrible state. It is a very different approach than traditional storytelling. Instead, Pixar storytellers begin by subtly putting the point of the story center stage but circling it. Then, throughout the story, revealing the point, and then finally, in the end, allowing readers to conclude that there was only one purpose in this entire story, it was inevitable.

The role of having a point and building up to that point is discussed in Chapter 2, where science rules storytelling. By building up to a point, the way that master storytellers do, they can perpetuate anticipation and boost the engagement, focus, and memory of their audience.

Heading back to the example, you realize that the point is about the state of the Earth, not Wall-e. And what happens? The humans clean up the Earth. However, they would never have gotten to that point without Wall-e. You want to achieve this full-circle effect, and you can only accomplish that by thoroughly understanding your point before you get started.

Common points in storytelling can include:

• Making a sale or gaining a customer

• Declaring your stance on a hot topic issue

• Giving resolution or insight to a well-known public event

• Sharing an experience with your audience to build a specific relationship, such as a spousal relationship or friendship

If you are still stuck on finding your point, consider completing these sentences:

1. I want to tell this story because _____.

2. The readers need to hear this story so they stop/start _____.

3. After sharing this story, I can _____.

4. After hearing this story, the listeners should _____.

5. This story shared human experiences, such as _____ and _____.

Through these five questions, you should have a pretty clear understanding of what you want to see come out of this story and what your point in telling it is.

Step Two: Define Your Character and Narrator

In storytelling, there is no rule on characters or the narrator. However, there are general common ways of handling both. First, you have personal stories told through the first person. Then, you have all the other stories.

When you are telling a personal story through the first person, it is generally easier to understand your character and narrator. Clearly, you know your character; it's you. But with the voice of narration, you need to determine if you are telling the story with all the knowledge you have now, or if you're starting as though you had no idea what was to come.

To see this in action, you might compare David JP Phillip's telling of his stillborn child—in his TEDx Talk, "The Magic of Storytelling"—to the narrator Scout from *To Kill a Mockingbird*. When Phillips talks about his loss, he begins the story with two unsuspecting parents of a five-year-old boy. The family is expecting a second child, and the tense of this retelling is past tense, which is the verb choice for most storytelling. However, he does not give insight into the fact that *he* has already lived through the events. Whereas in *To Kill a Mockingbird*, the narrator and character Scout is retelling events that *happened* to her within the confines of fiction. She tells readers directly on the first page, "... When enough years had gone by to enable us to look back on them, we sometimes discussed the events leading to his accident." This sentence is the narrator and primary character telling her audience directly that she would be telling them the events with the hindsight of an adult. However, the story took place during her childhood.

Those are the elements you need to consider when defining your character and narrator. Now, if you are working with a non-personal story, or a personal story told in the third person, you need to give more attention to character development. If a story starts and ends without any change to the primary character, the audience will be largely disappointed. Answer these questions about your primary character:

- What struggle or stasis is your character experiencing in the beginning?
- How do the events of the climax of the story affect them, and how do they change because of these events?
- How would your character follow up on those events?
- Will you share your character's inner thoughts?
- How do you identify with your character? - Is it you with a different name or someone else entirely? Do you like them?

To help define the scope of your narrator ask these questions:

- Is your narrator the character or a different entity? - Both are common occurrences.
- Is your narrator allowed to interject their opinion? - Popular among public speaking storytelling.
- What are the differences in education/knowledge, etc., between your narrator and your characters?

Step Three: Prepare to Write Authentically

Every storyteller has plenty of fears about the process of crafting and how to approach their story when it comes to actually sitting down and writing. You are not alone if you worry that someone will read your story and feel you have outed them somehow. You're not the only writer who feels that sharing a story could expose some inner part of yourself that you would rather keep private. You're also not alone in wondering if, as a storyteller, you do not have much to give. Many experience these fears with storytelling and writing, and if you don't experience them, you're lucky.

One of the most critical elements of your first draft is about your dedication to authenticity. Every story has a first draft, even if you are only sharing stories orally, getting them onto paper is vital. When you go through the act of writing, you can visually monitor the ebb and flow of your story, watching the characters, and seeing the point of your story become more present in each sentence. Remember that you will probably be the only person in the world to see this first draft. Be authentic and as honest as possible. It is important to briefly touch on how authenticity, and the current trend of "becoming authentic" are different from honesty.

There is this ongoing argument about authenticity and that people must learn to become or embrace their authentic selves. The truth is that you are yourself, and if you put on a different face or showcase a different side of your personality, that is still *you* being yourself.

When writing, be as authentic and raw as possible. If you are talking about your family, refer to them by name or as "Mom" and "Dad." You can always go through and edit to give them names as characters later. Many storytellers do, some don't. It might seem as though people are not authentic when they give an insincere compliment, but are they not being authentic to their desire to spare a person's feelings? You're going to be authentic no matter what, so you might as well just do what you want without the filter of believing that other people will judge or criticize. You have many sides and different aspects of your personality, and those may not always align perfectly. While you're writing your first draft, put the specifics of your values and personality as much to the side as possible, and instead focus on creating what feels right.

So how can you be authentic, and how do you know if you are authentic? The only question that matters is: Are you honest with yourself?

Honesty, on the other hand, is another issue, and it is an audience-based issue. Where authenticity may be lying to yourself, general honesty focuses on your honesty with the facts of the events. An audience can tell when the storyteller is outright lying, but storytellers may embellish or add emphasis on certain events to enhance the storytelling experience. Imagine an embellishment as adding a dash of salt onto your story. Whereas lying about events is serving chili and calling it mashed potatoes.

This book will leave you in control of honesty and now focus on the authenticity element because it is something that many storytellers struggle to manage. Here are a handful of tips to help build and test authenticity as you are writing.

• *Stuck in your story?* - Evoke the senses. If you're not sure about the authenticity during your retelling, tell what you saw, smelled, felt, heard, and tasted.

The senses can awake and shock the storyteller as well as the audience. For example, most adults have experienced a breakup. When telling a story about a breakup, you might share the heartache, the desire to eat anything in the fridge, or nothing at all. However, that is all surface-level detail; you are not giving yourself permission to stretch into that level of openness that is authentic to you. You're lying to yourself by saying, "Oh, this breakup was so bad that I ate a pint of ice cream." But if you delve into the senses, you can surprise yourself. You can say, "My body felt hot, and everything was blurry from tears while my throat was dry, and my tongue felt too big for my mouth. To say I was a mess would have been a drastic understatement."

• *Stop judging yourself* - That inner critic is the death of many great storytellers. Turn it off. Whenever you have a judgmental thought, consider it an internalized fear that will never become real, just like most other worries.

Your memories and ideas are unique to you, and there is nothing that should stop you from at least recording them. Now you may decide that some stories are not for sharing for a variety of reasons.

But with the goal of authenticity in mind, you should never stop yourself from writing the story. It's possible to tell these stories that you're most afraid of in a different context. Not every personal story has to be told in the first person. You can create a character version of yourself, but that is later in the editing process. For now, accept that you and everyone else on Earth have done embarrassing things, and experienced unjustified fear or worry. You're not alone, and the inner critic saying, "This is dumb" should not stop you from sharing a story. Rise above it.

- *Get involved in a workshop* – Finding a workshop or writing partner can help you push past that initial boundary of comfort. What you tell in public, the filtered and overedited version can improve when you have someone pushing you to do better.

Finding a workshop is pretty easy, as you can find many online. There are workshop podcasts that you can follow, and nearly all community colleges have writing workshops. When you have someone to talk to physically, you can have those difficult conversations that become difficult revelations in stories and, eventually, life-changing stories.

Step Four: Structure with Freytag's Pyramid

Your story must have a beginning, a middle, and an end. It is not really negotiable. Freytag's Pyramid is something that most people learn in school, and it's the basic triangle structure used to govern the storytelling format. Basically, there should be a beginning, and then some things should happen that naturally lead to the climax, then some things should wind down the story to deliver it to a satisfying ending.

However, that is all much easier said than done. Your favorite book, movie, and story all follow this structure to some degree. How can you execute on the same level? When you understand the function of each point on Freytag's Pyramid, you can create a more comprehensive outline that should produce a highly functional and engaging story.

1. Introduction

The introduction exists to deliver the necessary backstory and exciting force. If you cannot captivate your audience quickly, you need to work on this part in particular. You'll be working largely with exposition through this section by introducing the important characters, maybe setting the time period, and the tone.

In the beginning, you will give your audience:

- Information on whether this story is sad, happy, funny, dramatic, etc.
- Who is most important to the story.
- Hints as to the major changes ahead of these characters.
- The outside force that's impacting the main character or protagonist, the exciting force.

2. Rising Action

After the initial thing happens to the primary character, you have to keep going. What happens next? You might introduce more characters, change locations, or similar. The rising action is where you can build anticipation, which would prompt all those good story hormones discussed in Chapter 2. This is often the longest part of the story.

To see rising action in motion, look at the story of *Goldilocks and the Three Bears*. The introduction announces that Goldilocks went for a walk in a nearby forest and came upon a house. Most everything after that is rising action. The rising action in the Goldilocks story includes:

- Goldilocks tries all three porridges.
- Goldilocks tries all three chairs and breaks the baby bear's bed.
- Goldilocks tries all three beds and falls asleep in baby bear's bed.

Goldilocks trying out all three different things is the bulk of the story. It is what she does, and it perpetuates the feeling of safety and security that no one is home. In fact, Goldilocks gets so comfortable that she falls asleep. The rising action naturally follows the introduction and naturally leads to the climax, but is still tantalizing enough that the climax is exciting.

3. Climax

This is not usually very long, which means that every sentence must serve a specific and direct purpose. This is where things really change on a grander scale. The climax of the story is when the three bears return home to find Goldilocks. It is when Simba decides to return home, and it's when Snow White bites that poisoned apple. The climax is often much further along into the story than people initially imagine. So do not get discouraged if it seems like you are taking a while to get there.

In the clearest way possible: The climax is the point in the story where the beginning and the end start to reflect each other.

What that means is that during the climax, everything is on fire, it is alight, and burning brilliantly. All the values, themes, and character struggle given in the rising action will now be undone.

4. Falling Action

Now, things are devolving. They are not falling apart—though it can happen. Instead, often the actions are leading toward the only natural conclusion. Returning to Goldilocks, there are about two lines of falling action.

"And she jumped up and ran out of the room. Goldilocks ran down the stairs, opened the door, and ran away into the forest."

Goldilocks has a very tidy falling action in that everything is undone exactly. She leaves the house and goes back into the forest where she started. However, the well-known story of *Romeo and Juliet* has a slightly stickier falling action. At the climax, Juliet decides to fake her death so she could live the life she wants rather than marry Paris.

Romeo and Juliet's falling action includes:

- Juliet drinks the fake poison.

- Romeo drinks real poison.
- Juliet awakes and realizes their grave mistake and then kills herself.

But what is just as clear here is that the beginning is *undone* in the sense that these families would not stop fighting, but then their two teens made a choice together—leading to the natural conclusion of the fighting between the families as they share in the grief. It is a transition and a mirror.

It's very likely that as you write your falling action, it will feel like a lot of action in a short stretch of time. That's very common; do not shy away from it because, at this point, you are delivering on all the "promises" you made to your audience during that anticipation-building rising action section.

5. Conclusion or Catastrophe

There is the natural conclusion to the story, which should be satisfying and conclusive. Do not leave your audiences with a cliffhanger. Now, if your story hasn't really "ended" yet, give a "right now" conclusion. How have you or your character changed in viewpoint, perspective, and will that continue?

As you go through your conclusion, the audience must realize that the end is a result of the character, not the surrounding actions. In David JP Phillips's story about the loss of his baby, he concluded that it is still hard; it's an ongoing struggle. However, the biggest question that he faced after learning about the lack of a heartbeat, was not how he and his wife would go on, but what they would tell their son. That was the perspective change. The pregnancy wasn't just about them; they were second-time parents, so a third person was involved who simply could not be asked to understand this situation. It was literally the undoing of the introduction, which started with him talking about how excited his five-year-old son was about the upcoming sibling.

Now look through a handful of story conclusions that should be both familiar and reasonably satisfying:

- Rapunzel isn't locked in the tower anymore.
- Snow White is awakened by a prince and rescued from a terrible fate.
- Goldilocks decides never to return to that house in the woods.
- Rumpelstiltskin is found out, and the queen is released from his contract.

Step Five: Edit for Clarity and Connection

This part of the crafting process is difficult because many people feel as though they should be done. They write the story and then realize they need to do it again. Then, they have to edit again and again. So how can you edit for clarity, and can you be efficient when editing? Editing is part of the crafting process, and it is vital for good storytelling. Imagine if as soon as a slat of wood was propped onto four smaller pieces of wood, the carpenter called it a table. Or if the moment the batter was put in the oven, a baker called it a cake.

Editing can be fun, and it can inspire you to write even more. It is an opportunity to see how much you have developed as a storyteller. It's also the chance to rehearse your story if you are going to use it in a public forum.

"The first draft is just you, telling yourself the story." - Terry Pratchett

"If it's not right, keep editing until it is." - Curtis Tyrone Jones

There is a lot of freedom when it comes to editing your story. First, you do not have to edit from start to finish. You also don't have to edit against strict rules besides basic grammar functions. Finally, editing is subjective. If it is good, then good, but it doesn't have to be perfect. Remember that no story is perfect, and it's possible to overedit.

Here are Questions to Ask Yourself as you Edit

- Is this the most emotionally impactful way I could say this line/paragraph/etc.?

- Does this line connect with the audience?

- Is this clear? (Top tip: Read your story aloud; it's also a great rehearsal for public speaking!)

- Does this line or point in the story have a purpose that connects with the greater point of the story?

Of course, you need to edit for grammar, and not everyone is an expert on this. If you are going to deliver your story through a speech, presentation, ad, or public forum, this is less of an issue, but it's still something that deserves attention. For anyone who is not an expert with grammar, check out these tools:

- Hemingway App

- ProWritingAid (an online service that has both free and paid options)

- Grammarly

Special Notes on Visual Elements of Story Crafting

If you are telling your story in public, via TEDx, YouTube, in a classroom, business meeting, or even in an ad, then look for other elements to edit. How will you tell your story? With physical movement or visual aids? A slideshow or animation? Maybe actors will portray your story in an ad or short film. Maybe you will pace back and forth on a stage. Although this book will discuss the multiple mediums and delivery of a good story later, keep the beats of the story in mind, as you edit, to make the managing physical presentation easier later.

Chapter 5: Five Elements of a Good Story

What makes one story drastically different from another in terms of quality? Is a story good simply because of its content? No. Without a doubt, some of the most widely shared stories in the world arguably do not have the best content or even subject. However, there are some things that great stories share. It is surprising, but the tales of David and Goliath, *The Three Little Pigs*, *Lord of the Flies*, *The Boy Who Cried Wolf*, and La Llorona share common elements, although they range in genres—from a coming-of-age story to a hero-based epic to commonplace European folklore, to a scary ghost story.

The elements discussed here do not come with set rules. While there are "right" and "wrong" ways of presenting certain elements of a story, there are always times when a storyteller can break the rules. For example, one rule that you might choose to break is the "show don't tell" rule, and breaking that could be done for efficiency, or pacing, or to jump forward to more important information. These ten elements will be detailed at length, to help you know how and when to explore the opportunity of moving away from the standardized practices of each element.

The Ten Elements of a Good Story Include

1. Evocation or "Show Don't Tell."
2. Characters
3. A clear goal
4. Tension and conflict
5. Theme
6. Point of view or perspective
7. Symbolism
8. Morals
9. Resolution
10. A neatly tied bow

Anton Chekhov was a famous storyteller who wrote novels, plays, poetry, short stories, comic satire, and more. His quote changed the way that people viewed storytelling and crafting:

"Don't tell me the moon is shining; show me the glint of light on broken glass."

So what does evocation mean? Evocation is the act of bringing up or recalling a memory, feeling, sensation, or image into the conscious mind. Recall in Chapter 2, how stories should cause multiple centers of the brain to interact. One of those centers should be a memory center. So, evocation plays that role in storytelling. It is the word you assign to that trigger, which should prompt the memory portion of the brain to communicate with the language processing and the endocrine system. Science has not confirmed that evocation is one of the most significant elements of good storytelling. Nevertheless, how do you do this? How do you evoke emotion?

How to Accomplish This

1. *Use active verbs to portray the five senses*

   a. Example one: "Crunching from across the room pushed my heart rate up, a headache pounding against my temples."

    b. Example two: "My hands were black with coal dust. The grime rolled over my forehead, mingling with sweat."

2. *Be bold*

    a. Example one: "Mount Everest was unforgiving. The snow didn't flurry; it howled. The ice didn't form; it consumed."

    b. Example two: "Audience screams from behind piercing black nothing. Blinding lights flashed, leaving spots across my recovering vision."

3. *Remove the sticky words (and, the, in, of, etc.) or keep it short and sweet*

    a. Example one: "The sun warmed her skin."

    b. Example two: "Hot pasta hit my tongue, searing taste buds off."

4. *Dialogue with your audience (for public speakers and marketers)*

    a. Example one: "Would you raise your eyebrow when faced with the question of..."

    b. Example two: "You can't do that. Normal people don't do that!"

5. *Overwhelm with movement*

    a. Example one: "I switched off the light, went down the hall, walked into the kitchen, and..."

    b. Example two: "The boy slept, drilled, and painted for hours, again and again."

Typically, this element applies most to storytellers who are writing novels. It also plays a large role for public speakers, teachers, and, most importantly, businesses. The difference is that in various mediums, you will face different challenges and receive different benefits.

When You Can Explore Alternatives

Sometimes showing is not as efficient as telling, and if you are referring to the backstory or purely informative content, then you can likely tell your reader. Although using shorter sentences is a great way to show, many storytellers find themselves fluffing their stories with tons and tons of description in an effort to show their readers what is happening.

When deciding if you should just tell your audience, consider the surrounding material. Always show through the most important parts of the story, and then tell when you need to manage your time, pacing, or character development better. There are times when you must sacrifice one good element of a story for another, but it is a decision you need to weigh carefully.

Characters

Every good story needs characters, but who they are and how you portray them can derail the story or set it on the right course. How do you know whether you have a good character or not? Well, it is not about them being "good" or "bad." It's all about how you build the story with them in mind.

Many people mistakenly think that telling a personal story will make this much easier. However, when detailing a personal injury, you must carefully reflect on your behavior and what thoughts guided your decision making, taking you from where you were to where you are now.

Great Characters Have

- A clear goal
- Fear, anxiety, or worry
- Human flaws (they pick their teeth, apologize too often, and have nervous ticks)
- A background
- Unique combinations of personality traits (extraversion, neuroticism, openness, etc.)
- Relatable qualities
- Susceptibility to both success and failure

- Perspective on life (characters have opinions on social structure, relationships, education, political beliefs, upbringing, and more.)
- An attitude: pessimistic, realistic, or optimistic
- Intuition

When You Can Explore Alternatives

Can you ever have a flat character? Well, Charles Dickens, one of the top storytellers of his time, relied on flat characters. However, he used them in a way you would use pawns in chess. If you can execute a flat character on that level, hat's off to you, but be careful not to commit too much attention to these flat characters. Many storytellers now will rely on a trope to give an identity to a flat character.

An example of a storyteller giving a personal story to a crowd, involving a flat character, might be:

"My mom, she was a fall-down drunk, at least until my 20th birthday. I haven't seen her since then. But my dad, he was always there, always present. Every soccer game, graduation, promotion, he was there for us kids."

Now, the mom is a character in this story. She has no goal or directive, but with the short phrase "fall-down drunk," you can assume that she is not dedicated to her kids, which is the critical purpose of her presence in the story. Not every character has to be extremely developed, but there is no reason to have characters that lack personality.

A clear goal

Having a clear goal is not about the point or theme of your story. Instead, it is about the end game, what will happen to the character. Sometimes that goal is not always so apparent, and that is where you start to lose an audience or listeners. A great place to see this in action is in marketing because often commercials have twenty seconds or fewer, excluding internet ads and "trailers." How can you see storytelling in action, in such a short amount of time, executed well?

A really fun example of this is the Pepsi "More Than OK" commercial. It starts in a diner where a woman orders a Coke, and the waiter asks, "Is Pepsi okay?" Right from the start, you have a clear goal. You know this is a Pepsi commercial, and that they are making fun of a common phrase, which infers that they're second to Coca-Cola. Then Steve Carrell jumps out and asks questions like, "Is the laughter of a child, okay?" Then he jumps to others who are not saying okay with gusto until Lil John and Cardi B jump in with their spins on how to say, "Okay." Finally, the woman looks around and says, "I want a Pepsi." The goal was clear, they followed up on it, and it played into this woman realizing that she doesn't want Coke; she wants Pepsi.

Another variance of this story is *The Gift of the Magi* by O. Henry. It is mandatory reading for most high schoolers, and the tale revolves exclusively around two people with the same goal. They want to give their special someone (each other) an outstanding and meaningful gift. There is very little else going on in this story, and it's compelling because every action moves the characters closer to their goals.

How to Accomplish This

1. *Determine if the goal is external, internal, or a mix of both*

In *The Gift of the Magi*, the goal was external but had an internal motivation. Throughout the story, they made the internal motivation clear by expressing the feelings of those involved. In storytelling, particularly public storytelling, you often do not have that much time. Remember: the more nuanced the goal, the longer the story.

2. *Start your story with the goal in plain sight*

This goes right back to the evocation element. You can communicate a goal that your character has without outright saying, "I want to buy my wife a gift." However, it is up to you to decide how you present your goal. When Kathleen Baty starts her story about her stalker, she usually begins with something along the lines of, "I tried for more than ten years to get away from this guy." Which initially might seem like she cannot get out of a bad relationship. Then, the next line is often about how the police could not help because he hadn't technically done anything illegal, and it did not matter if she moved, or what school she transferred to. He was always there. She puts her story in plain sight while presenting the facts about the information rather than saying, "I was stalked for more than ten years, and I'm here to tell you all about it."

3. *Emphasis on the important*

When you have the opportunity to share a story, especially in front of an audience, you must know what parts are the most important. Although you have the opportunity to write your story and edit until you are comfortable, you want to make sure that your audience can differentiate between key information and the remainder of the story.

Now, it is easy to say that everything is important because one action feeds into another, and that feeds into another that beats into another. However, the most critical elements of the story are not always the ones in plain sight. Going back to the example used above from *The Gift of the Magi*, the most important part of the story is not the gift at all; it is the sacrifice that both people make. Often the essential element comes from backstory or a personality aspect of the primary character. That is what you need to focus on when you emphasize different pieces of the story.

Activity

To test your ability to emphasize the importance, here is a fun activity. Take the story of *Little Red Riding Hood* and change the most important element of the story. Now keep in mind the most significant element is not that Little Red Riding Hood stopped and talked to the Big Bad Wolf, or how she was fooled when the Wolf had posed as her grandmother. The important element is that Red is a dutiful grandchild, but had a moment of lapsed judgment. After all, the red velvet cape was made by her grandmother, and Red loved it so much that she refused to take it off.

So change that most critical element. What if Red was not so dutiful? Or what if she was still dutiful but less loving? It would remove the scene of her stopping to pick the flowers, which would eliminate the Wolf's involvement. *Little Red Riding Hood* is not a story that sits well with you, and you can do this exercise with almost any folktale.

Change the most important element of the story or change the emphasis and place it in a different spot, and you will see a drastically different version of events.

When You Can Explore Alternatives

When exploring alternatives, you take the risk of becoming an unreliable narrator. Now, this goes far beyond having an occasional Red Herring or sudden twist in the story. Instead, what you are looking at is the high probability of losing all the trust you have built with your audience.

Unreliable narrators are seen in *Fight Club* and *Forrest Gump*. These stories are acceptable to an audience, and the unreliability of the narrator is killed by something that the narrator also cannot control; one case is a mental disorder, and the other is a low IQ.

Some public storytellers choose to be unreliable narrators, and they often give a warning when they do. A popular podcast called **RISK!** encourages people to come forth with personal stories and share them through the art of storytelling. One storyteller recounted through the podcast an episode of mania. He started his story by saying that he experiences manic episodes and that he was not in control of his actions during those episodes. He also explained at the beginning of his story that after a manic episode, he often does not remember anything. That sentence alone tells the audience that everything that he shares about his manic episode could be a lie or a false memory, or it could be true. Did it make the story less compelling or less entertaining? No.

4. *Tension and conflict*

Imagine that you come home after a hard day's work, are tired and hungry, and your spouse asks how your day was? But you know this question is not about your day because your spouse wants to tell you about their day. They want to tell you about changes in procedure or their meeting, or the drive home. There is a reason why people don't care about these everyday stories. There is no tension. There's no conflict!

"On a sunny morning, I walked into my kitchen, opened the refrigerator door, and grabbed the last gallon of milk. While the coffee was brewing, I searched around for sugar and a spoon. Then I finally mixed my morning cup."

This is a terrible story. There is no tension or conflict, despite how it has a beginning, middle, and end. Would you be happy if you attended an event, and that is what the speaker had to say? What if your boss told that story at the next meeting? You would be bored out of your mind.

What people crave from a story are tension and conflict, but they get picky. Generally, you want a very delicate balance between the two. If you have too much tension, then you lose your audience because there is no payoff. While if you have too much conflict, you lose your audience because it is just too frustrating to experience.

How to Accomplish a Balance of Tension and Conflict with Everything Else

There are four types of conflict when it comes to storytelling and literature. With storytelling, however, again, you have a time constraint, and you simply do not have hours and hours to lay the foundation for your conflict. Keep that in mind as you determine what type of conflict fits your story.

- Man vs. man
- Man vs. nature
- Man vs. self

- Man vs. the system

So the story of the Waco Texas and the Branch Davidians would fall into the Man vs. the system conflict. There were other people involved and making decisions, but ultimately it was people versus the government. The same is easy to say for the American Revolutionary War.

Hatchet, a Young Adult classic novel, is man vs. nature. While a speaker recounting her experiences with depression and anxiety would be man vs. self, and a battle between a hero and a villain is man vs. man.

Understanding the setup of your conflict can ensure that you do not overload your audience with tension and set yourself up for failure. If you have a man vs. self-conflict, you don't want to focus or emphasize the arguments with other people, the struggle against the government, and how Mother Nature hates the main character. Instead, you put those other challenges through the lens of the first conflict. The fights a person has with other people when they have an inner struggle are often a result of that inner struggle or a symptom of that struggle, such as a bad mood.

When You Can Explore Alternatives

There really are no alternatives to including the conflict in your story. Even stories as basic as *The Very Hungry Caterpillar* have conflict. People are taught from an early age that any story worth telling has some type of conflict, and to emphasize that conflict, you must include tension. This is one of the few elements of storytelling that if you are missing it, you probably do not have a full story.

5. *Theme*

David Lieber, a famous columnist and now public speaker, talked about his experience of moving to Texas in the early 1990s on a well-known TEDx talk. The underlying theme is connectivity and getting to know your fellow person, and creating change in the world through connection and storytelling. He starts by talking about the series of questions that Texans ask when they first meet people, all of which he gives the wrong answers. But he was playing with his point, and he allowed his theme to continue uninterrupted. Then he uses that story to connect directly with his audience. It didn't matter that he gave the same wrong answers to every Texan he met. What mattered and what came through with his story was his theme of that desire to connect with another person.

The theme can be all manner of things because you can have the radical extent of *Animal Farm*, with the theme being the Russian Bolshevik Revolution, and then *The Very Hungry Caterpillar*, with a theme that revolves around self-care and growth.

How to Use the Theme in Your Story

The theme is used via thorough development and careful construction of your plot—and you don't need tens of thousands of words to accomplish this. You can still see it through the character actions, the narrator's tone, and the sequence of events.

To get a visual element of the theme's role in storytelling, use the association between the plot and Freytag's pyramid. The plot is depicted in a triangular or pyramid structure; the role of the theme is more of a spiderweb. The theme carefully weaves between plot points, characters, conflict, and the overall point of the story.

Be purposeful with your theme. There are many universal themes, including the battle of good over evil and growing powerful without growing wicked. Many universal themes cover human nature or the plight of human existence. Generally, universal themes are a little easier for first-time storytellers because they have probably experienced them often in their own lives.

Aside from being purposeful when choosing your theme, the only advice for implementing a theme within your story is to identify moments of opportunity within your plot. The best way to explain this is through an example, such as *The Boy Who Cried Wolf*. This book will go through the major plot points and explain how the theme correlates, but first, it will explain how the primary theme of the story is not to lie, and the secondary theme is that nobody believes a liar.

- The boy is bored and shouts, "Wolf! Wolf!" – The first lie (theme)
- A villager tells him, "Don't cry wolf if there's no wolf." – Importance of the truth
- The boy lies again – The second lie
- The villagers get angry at him – The emphasis of consequences for lying
- Real wolf comes in – The Truth!
- Villages don't respond – Consequence of lies
- Sheep are eaten – Consequence of the lies

When You Can Explore Alternatives

In theory, it is nearly impossible to tell a story that does not have a theme. If you were to do so, you would have to go way out of your way to manage it. There is always some underlying theme, such as someone accomplishing a great feat or showing that opposites attract.

While some of these elements are possible to avoid, many like theme and characters are just impossible to avoid. These are the elements of making a decent story good or a good story great! Explore each and their possible roles in your story to improve it and build your storytelling skills. As you advance, you can add other elements, such as symbolism, unique perspective, and morals. However, when you are crafting your first story, you should focus on these five elements along with your structure and then an authentic tone.

Chapter 6: Storytelling in Public Speaking

Most of the storytelling that happens is through the medium of public speaking. That can happen when you are talking to your team, addressing people in an audience, or connecting face to face with customers. Maybe you're aspiring to become a professional speaker or a professional storyteller. It is all possible and a reasonable career choice. However, no matter your career choice, it's extremely likely that you will need to public speak at some point. When doing that, if you're trying to make a compelling point, you should approach public speaking with storytelling.

Your public speaking does not have to be a dreadful or dry event. Most people don't look forward to public speaking because they feel as though the audience has already decided on the matter. If people have shown up, they have done so for a good time or because they are required to. On a large scale, indeed, some people have already decided their opinion on hot topic issues. Additionally, many show up to conferences or conventions either because they like the speaker or because it's part of their job. Note that as you prepare for your public speaking event and how you can implement storytelling, you really have much more control—over the audience's experience—than you think.

Approaching storytelling, knowing that you are going to have to deliver the story through a public speaking event, calls for attention to different elements of crafting the story. Public speaking is different from delivering a story through a video—that you can post on YouTube after editing it repeatedly—advertisement, or book.

How Is Public Speaking Different?

When questioning how public speaking is different from other mediums for storytelling, the most common answer is that you cannot have a conversation. In a book, video, or paper advertisement, you can present the idea of a conversation where the reader will insert themselves into one side and accept the development of that discussion. The argument is that you can't manipulate the characters into being both believable and authentic while carrying on a conversation with your audience—except that you can.

What are the best ways to implement a conversational tone? Begin your speech by knowing that your story applies to the entire audience. Everyone there is possibly your target audience, and they should all want to hear your story. However, on the other hand, you need to accept that people in this audience are going to have different viewpoints and different past experiences that affect their opinion on your particular topic.

In 2015, Tony Robbins gave a stage performance at the National Achievers Congress in Sydney, Australia. He talked about failure and had a conversation with his audience; in fact, he often has conversations with his audiences. He asked at the beginning of his public speaking event:

"Who here has ever failed?"

Of course, he received a huge response from people acknowledging that they had failed. He followed that with another question, and kept the conversation going:

"Why did you fail?"

The audience was tongue-tied.

So Robbins helped them out a bit.

"Okay, what did you use to say the reason you failed when you were bullshitting yourself?" So what excuse did the audience members use to explain why they failed?

He got a few different responses. The economy, the lack of technology, and similar responses were the "reasons" for failure. Then he moved onto a story about a TED Talk he did seven years earlier when he asked the same question, "Why did you fail?" At the TED event, Al Gore stood up and gave an answer for why he failed to become president—he didn't have enough Supreme Court justices. This part of the 2015 Sydney talk was momentous as it allowed Robbins to share a story about another conversation (with Al Gore) while engaging in an active conversation (with his current audience). It is an inception for conversation and storytelling.

You can surely have a conversation with your audience and control it. You can push your audience to get the answers that you need to move forward, but you can also use conversation to feed your story.

You have the opportunity to have a conversation, and if you miss that opportunity, you may not have an effective story. Your story could fall flat, and it could be the one missed opportunity that costs you the entire speech, the entire purpose that you got up there.

There is also a unique opportunity to be bigger physically. Moving with physical gestures and a clearer voice can make or break your story. Imagine you are telling the story of your mechanic grandfather, and are on stage or in front of an office and mime turning wrenches. It sounds ridiculous, but the physical element of storytelling is very important, especially when you're in front of a live audience.

One of the biggest differences between storytelling through public speaking and other forms is that you can be as physically involved as you want.

Start with a Bang

When you are in a public speaking forum, you have limited time to grab people's attention, and the clock starts ticking the second your feet hit the stage. If you're in a less controlled public speaking environment, you still need to drive forward that immediate impact. If you do not have your audience's attention within five seconds, you're floundering. Comics call it bombing, and it is exactly what it sounds like. Wondering what it feels like?

You stand up and walk in front of your peers. Everyone there knows you. They know that you are talking about the new training initiative and they have already decided they don't want to do more training. But you go up anyway. After clearing your throat and trying not to shuffle your feet, you look around. You tell them that training can improve sales, decrease costly mistakes, and help to create better employees that stick with the company longer. Your heart rate is up—you know this because your pulse is *thumping* in the back of your head as you see people checking their phones rather than taking notes. It's terrible and often happens because when you're public speaking, that initial story, that very beginning, needs to have an electrical charge that can shock the room.

Imagine if you walked in and said, in a very risky move, "When I first started, my training wasn't enough. Over time, I learned, but still, I hadn't had enough training to meet my sales quota/help customers/etc." That would have had a much larger impact than, "Way back when people didn't focus on training too much, everyone learned as they went along."

Starting with a bang is so drastic that you cannot give a soft introduction when speaking in public. Tony Robbins stands out as a public speaker because he makes his audience physically alert, he starts with a *bang*—well, jumping, but the same effect.

Start with the End in Mind

When you are not speaking publicly, you can edit your story until you get a nice tidy ending. However, with public speaking, your story will fluctuate slightly depending on the response from your audience and the purpose of that particular telling. So, to ensure that you get that same nice and tidy ending, you need to start by already knowing how you're going to end. You need to have a theme introduced right away and then give a conclusion on that same theme at the end. Here is an example of a story that could take a different turn but starts and ends the same way:

Example One

"Have any of you ever felt like Cinderella? I'd say don't get me started, but we're already here, aren't we? So every Sunday, I'm tidying the house, getting the meals ready for the week, and setting up everything for work and school for the kids the next day. Somewhere, usually around noon, I get that toxic voice in my head. The one that envisions my husband and children as the wicked stepmother and ugly stepsisters who force me to do all these chores. Every. Single. Week. And you know what? After a while, I believe it. I believe that there's no one else to do the work, that there's no other option. Until, of course, I cool down. I realize that I'm the one that demands the lunches be made ahead of time. I'm the one that insists on having the house clean and shoes by the door before Monday morning. I have no right to feel like Cinderella if I'm not going to be cheerful about all these chores. Especially if they're self-inflicted."

Example Two

"Have any of you felt like Cinderella? Here's what happens in my house. Every Sunday, I clean, cook, and prepare for the week ahead. During that time, I focus on all the bad. It is almost cathartic. Almost. While for the rest of the week, I can go through the household duties as Cinderella does with a good attitude and smile, Sunday just isn't possible. I become overwhelmed by all those irritating feelings against the others in my house—the ugly stepsisters and stepmother—and then unleash them on Sunday. However, by Monday morning, I realize again that I don't have any right to feel like Cinderella. No one else ever told me that I had to do all this work on one day of the week. I feel like Cinderella, but the truth is, this is all from me."

Both versions circled to the same revelation and the same beginning. The story has the same message and is roughly the same length. But the storyteller could alter either version depending on the audience. *Example One* has a touch of humor, whereas *Example Two* had more introspection and seriousness.

Don't Say "Um" - Pause and Take a Breath

When people tell stories, their minds need a moment to process what they are doing while also watching the audience and adapting as necessary. That is when they say "um," "so," or any variety of other filler words. Instead, they should fight this urge to say "um" and just pause. Some of the world's best public speakers will pause for as much as three seconds or even longer. When you are standing in front of an audience, three seconds is a long time.

Taking a breath or pausing is not the end of your speech. It does not mean that you are losing the conversational floor; it means that your brain is doing what brains do. Knowing that the best public speakers in the world take pauses and breaks is a substantial relief. People think much faster than they can speak, and they must take the time to think about what they say. If you're speaking in public, it's better to pause than ramble, stutter, or say "um" a hundred times.

Make Sure Your Physical Presence is Captivating

There are a few times that you need to be very conscious of your physical stance and traits. Public speaking is one of those times. If you tend to shove your hands in your pocket, hang your head, or hunch your shoulders, you need to do some physical rehearsing. Even if you do not have obvious nervous habits, it is best to rehearse your speed again and again physically.

By rehearse, this means without a script or prompt, just telling your story in a wide-open space. Pace the floor, talk with your hands, and explore how you can naturally connect with the audience by using your body. Unfortunately, there is no complete guidebook to this because while fist-pumping might be natural for one person, it will be awkward and forced for another. Do what feels right for you. But avoid these common habits:

- Wringing your hands
- Brushing the hair from your face
- Touching the back of your neck
- Brushing your hands against your pants
- Pulling your shoulders forward
- Slouching

When it comes to public speaking and storytelling, you have a lot of freedom. You can tell multiple stories, stand-alone stories, and engage in active conversation. It is an immersive experience for your audience if you deliver your story with an outstanding connection. That is what public speaking comes down to—connecting with your audience, connecting the beginning and end of your story, and connecting your audience with the points of your story. Use the techniques mentioned above to ensure that you are adapting to your audience and presenting yourself (and your story) in the best manner possible.

Chapter 7: Storyselling: Storytelling as a Marketing Tool

Storytelling and storyselling are not necessarily the same thing. However, before you write off this chapter as irrelevant to anyone that is not a marketer, keep in mind that everyone participates in marketing. There is the role of marketing creator and consumer, but other professionals require marketing and storyselling skills to build their careers in different ways than just making a sale. Getting a buy-in and obtaining support for changes, building a brand, or even teaching others can all happen through storyselling.

Storytelling is the act of emotionally conveying information or an account to others. Now, in marketing, you see this often; in fact, marketers have relied on an emotional response for decades. However, storytelling marketing is not enough to stand on its own. You simply cannot get up on a stage or film a YouTube video and tell your brand's story; you also need to market that story, your brand, and yourself. Without something to tie that story to, your brand's story is just a story. It's not a marketing tool, it's not an ambassador for your brand, and it's not going to help your business.

Storyselling, however, aims to accomplish those things. You can change your storytelling marketing plan to an effective storyselling plan through a combination of storytelling and data-driven marketing. It takes the foundation of storytelling and blends it with marketing principles for effective conversion and engagement.

Through the act of storyselling, you can captivate your target customer base, engage your current customers, and build brand loyalty when very few customers are willing to give brand loyalty.

What is Storyselling?

Storyselling is the combination of storytelling and data-driven marketing with the explicit purpose of boosting sales and gaining a greater portion of your target market. Accomplishing this through storytelling requires that you devote much more attention to marketing copy.

Now, storyselling calls several technical questions to attention. Take the time to answer these questions to build the foundation of your storyselling platform.

1. Will you have one ongoing story or a different story for each marketing campaign?

2. Will you have a consistent narrator, character, or speaker?

3. Is your story a personal one, or is your story the account of your market?

4. How can you use the stories meaningful to your brand in a meaningful way to your target audience?

5. How will you track the progress and success of your storyselling campaign or branding?

These can all have drastically different answers, so this is something that you have to evaluate carefully. If you are working as an entrepreneur or with a marketing team, you need to look at the best answers to these questions for your customers and what is best for your brand.

Storyselling is unique in that there is so much more flexibility than simple data-driven marketing techniques. Without diving into an overly complicated example, take a quick look at Disney. Disney is among the oldest brands to actively use storyselling, which makes sense because they were unmatched in storytelling for decades.

As of November 15, 1965, Disneyland became "The Happiest Place on Earth." Think about it for a minute because, in that one line, they begin what would evolve into a decades-long tale of a story about all the Disney lovers around the world. They perpetuate that concept and core of their storyselling with commercials that show the initial "wow" factor of a child seeing Disney's Main Street for the first time, or a teenager exploring the Epcot theme park. Disney uses these flashes of moments to share the stories that happen in their parks every day. A man gets down on one knee in Disney Paris, and an ecstatic woman across from him jumps up and down. People have seen these commercials for decades, and countless more people have experienced or witnessed these stories firsthand.

A peek into the technical elements of Disney's storyselling:

- The stories come from the customers because of the experience. They're telling stories about Disneyland visitors.
- Disney doesn't sell movies or theme park tickets; they sell magic.
- They use multiple mediums for the same concept. They may run segmented marketing campaigns, but the magical experience of Disney is always at the core of the marketing message and story.

Consumers Want Storyselling

Not everyone is obsessed with a good commercial. Generally, if a consumer is going to watch a commercial, trailer, or view a print ad, they want something entertaining. Storyselling boosts conversions by over 30 percent, which aside from the early days of drip email marketing, few other marketing tactics have hit that level of success.

Additionally, B2B marketing almost exclusively relies on storyselling. Since storyselling became the new buzzword in the early 2010s, focused business-to-business companies have developed this marketing tactic better than nearly anyone else. Storyselling has become the top converting and most used marketing technique in B2B companies in 2017, and since then, it has stayed the most important marketing technique to these types of businesses.

But how much do consumers really want story-driven ads? Ninety-two percent of consumers want ads that give a story, rather than pitch right out of the gate. Marketing is about convincing your consumer that they want your product. To do that, you need to give them what they want, and the result has been countless companies developing story-driven marketing initiatives. But how can you reach customers and deliver a sales message along with a story? Is it possible to reach consumers in a way that is impactful and hits them when they are most susceptible to ads? With so many moving away from traditional cable and switching to ad-fewer streaming services, marketers are losing their access to customers.

How and Where to Deliver Stories to Consumers

When you are trying to use storyselling, you need to figure out your platform and medium for delivering the story. It won't necessarily change what story you tell, but it can change how you tell it. For example, if you decide to use an influencer to engage with customers, you have the opportunity for conversations directly with the target market. Influencers can talk with consumers; they can post hour-long videos of content that tells the story of the brand, and they can go out and meet people directly. Whereas if you are focusing on YouTube and Facebook ads, you have the limit of a twenty-second to three-minute-long video to convey your story.

The *where* part of this question will be answered first. You can deliver stories to your customers through:

- TV, streaming ads, and YouTube ads – video advertisement
- Social media – influencers
- Social media – brand management
- Radio engagement – interviews, talks, engaging with stations that suit your target market
- B2B networking events and conferences
- Philanthropic events that allow for speeches and public communication
- Email campaigns
- Company blog

Social media storytelling, particularly through influencers, has become a substantial part of marketing. One example is Jeffree Star, founder of the makeup brand bearing his name. He operates his own YouTube channel and happily shares the rags-to-riches story—that is his "how this all started" story. However, he will also post hour-long videos, telling the stories of his company's inner workings, for his followers. He uses his social media presence to tell stories, not just about himself, but the people in his life, business, and that ultimately make his business possible. Other brands do not necessarily post videos of very direct storytelling but instead use their social media presence to perpetuate their brand's narrative, which will be covered at the end of this chapter.

Now, moving onto the *how* elements, you need to review your business story carefully. How did you start your business, and why? Tell that story because it is vital to your brand and market. For companies that have a specific initiative, it can make the difference between people choosing your service or your competitors. You still want to convey a story, but you have so many ways to do it, that there are nearly limitless options. So, you need to start paring down the possibilities immediately. Use these starting points to generate ideas about implementing different types of storyselling:

- Create a "how we started" campaign (Bush's Beans, Chik-fil-A, Chewy, Blue Buffalo)
- Show your staff members enjoying their job and helping customers (Helpful Honda People, Target)
- Our customers love us story (Disney, Dairy Queen)
- The "we do it better" story (Liberty Mutual Insurance)
- The "we make things easier" story (Staples, Expedia, Alexa/Amazon)

Keep in mind that even when storyselling, the story you craft needs to be authentic and strike a chord with the audience. It is also an opportunity to emphasize the brand values, such as a humorous tone or a dedication to service. For example, Liberty Mutual uses storyselling in commercials that almost always have a funny edge. One commercial starts with a "normal" looking man talking to the camera, "Car insurance that won't replace the full value of the vehicle? You're better off throwing your wallet into the harbor." Of course, afterward, he realizes he did throw his wallet in, and now you have a funny story about a frustrated vehicle owner who got swindled on his insurance settlement and threw his wallet into the harbor. Then, the commercial turns to acknowledge that Liberty Mutual promises the full value of your car when it is totaled. They used a character, gave a scenario, added some humor, and closed out with a company promise. They told a meaningful and authentic story that many can identify with after a bad insurance settlement situation.

Resources for Storyselling

It is important to note, especially if you are an entrepreneur, that not all marketers are storytellers, and not all storytellers are marketers. Expect some room for development as your key person begins using these two very different skillsets together. Additionally, if you're building your brand, you need to learn how to use both storytelling and marketing tactics for effective storyselling. Eventually, within a brand that uses storytelling, you need not only your leadership team and marketers using storyselling, but also your sales and customer service teams supporting this side of the brand.

Arm your marketers with the tools that they need. For example, A Diamond is Forever does not stand on its own as a story. But with the entire marketing team building a vision of brides-to-be, proposals, and vow renewals, the 1948 De Beers ad still works and has transitioned from a slogan to a story. Ensure that there is a team of people working on developing characters, creating visuals or plot lines, and implementing conflict and growth into the stories you are using. Again, this only comes with the action of doing it. You cannot learn to create stories without actually sitting down and crafting them.

However, you need to ensure that your writing is clear, concise, and captivating. To do that, use these tools:

• ProWriting Aid - an online resource with both free and paid versions; it's great for editing grammar, structure, flow, and engagement.

• Grammarly - a subscription-based editing system that checks for grammar, readability, style, and more.

• People - you simply can't get better than a set of human eyes. Take your story to someone and ask them, does this work?

If you are stuck on the technical elements of crafting a story meant for marketing, then there are tools for that, too. You can order Bloomstein's BrandSort cards, which are fun prompt cards that give brand values, perspectives, pre-created characters, and more. The point of these types of tools is that they can get the creative juices flowing. Can you create an authentic story from prompt cards? No. But you can realize that your character is much less complicated than you initially thought, or that exploring a different perspective has made your story well rounded.

Special Notes for Marketers

Unlike storytelling that happens in churches, schools, and throughout public forums, marketers need a conclusive "end" that still brings many possibilities. The classic ending, "... and they lived happily ever after." is an example of this because there is not a clear picture of what happily ever after looks like. It is left to each person to explore that ending and draw their conclusions. However, accomplishing this with particular stories is a bit difficult. The "how we started" stories may seem hard to wrap-up because you're clearly still in business, so where do you end your story?

The key to an open-ended resolution is to end the one story of that commercial, print ad, or video and then perpetuate your tone and voice throughout all other brand narratives. Alignment with purpose throughout all brand communications is critical.

Chapter 8: Social Media and Influencer Storytelling

Influencers seem to have spawned from nowhere, but they've been decades in the making. From the time that celebrities began endorsing products, and appearing in commercials, the development of influencers was underway. Wheaties was well known for showing the best of athletes on their boxes with the narrative that these baseball and basketball players ate Wheaties. Did they really? Who knows, but kids everywhere wanted to eat the same cereal as Michael Jordon or Mary Lou Retton. The effectiveness of this type of marketing is ultimately what has led to the vast success of influencers, such as the Kardashians, Rosanna Pansino, and PewDiePie. Social media has made influencers more powerful than ever before, and unlike a few decades ago, they are not athletes or movie stars. These are professional influencers, a new breed of entertainer.

What the Pros on Digital Marketing Say About Influencers

Influencers have had such an impact on marketing that it is impossible to acknowledge their domination in social media and digital marketing. Many influencers have achieved celebrity status just by posting videos of themselves storytelling—or better phrased, storyselling.

To Run Through Some Quick Stats

- Seventy percent of teens trust social media influencers more than celebrities.
- Eighty-five percent of women rely on influencers and social media posts for shopping or purchasing advice.
- Forty-nine percent of consumers rely on influencers' recommendations, and 40 percent of them use Twitter, Instagram, and YouTube.
- Sixty percent of teens report following influencers and using their advice to try new things and products.
- The average ROI of an influencer campaign is $6.50 per dollar invested.

The full impact of influencers can be seen in the disaster of the Fyre Festival. One man used the power of influencers to stage a "luxury" summer festival experience that only the rich could experience. This person built up Fyre Festival with only influencer marketing, and through this scheme, he made 27.4 million dollars, while paying 5.2 million dollars to influencers, and not paying for booking shows or events, or arranging for the luxury experience he promised. Without influencers, this scam would have fallen apart, but influencers such as the Kardashian/Jenner group and various top models of the time perpetuated a narrative that they were much more involved in the development and involvement of Fyre Festival than they were. It was only after the disaster of people arriving for the festival to have no live music, and terrible living conditions, did people realize that these influencers are not often part of the company, just a marketing tool.

Influencer and Social Media Marketing are the Future – Tips for Using These Tools

From a survey of marketers, 22 percent agreed that influencers are the future of marketing because they are most cost-effective and can deliver high impact storyselling. Traditional marketers, however, also agreed that there are new foundations or principles that companies should consider when building their influencer campaigns. There is a way to choose the right type of influencer for your brand, and that is what it comes down to. You must always keep the focus on your brand, your company's story, and the story that is meaningful to your target market.

How to choose the right influencer for your brand is easier than you might imagine. Initially, you want to narrow down which influencers are present in your niche. It won't do to have a beauty influencer working with a restaurant brand. Always use an influencer that already works within your niche.

Then, decide what level of influencer you need. Of course, the higher the level, the more expensive their services. Here are the various levels and some insight into what you should expect from each degree:

- Mega influencers (Jeffrey Starr, the Kardashians, Michelle Lewin, Jake Paul):

Celebrity status, well known by people outside of their niche, and very expensive.

- Macro-influencers – between 100,000 and 1,000,000 followers.
- Micro-influencers – 1,000 to 100,000 followers:

This makes up 90 percent of influencer marketing agreements, and it works well because this level of influencers has exceptionally high authenticity. Their followers love them, and usually, they can have a crazy high impact in their local communities.

- Nano Influencers – fewer than 1,000:

These influencers can be huge if the influencer fits the niche. A small-parts home electronics engineer that hosts a channel or navigates social media as an influencer can have a massive impact in their niche even with less than 1,000 followers.

Successful Examples of Social Media and Influencer Storytelling

There is nothing more fun than looking at influencers matched with brands, both expected and unexpected. It is a great way to see storyselling in action alongside one of modern marketing's best tools.

Dunkin' Donuts – National Donut Day

On National Donut Day, Dunkin' Donuts used an ad campaign with eight popular influencers, including Skylar Bouchard, Aww Sam, Megan and Liz, Harris Heller, Corey Scherer, and Marcus Perez. They all showcased the campaign in their own way, which is exactly what influencers do. Skylar Bouchard, for example, showed off a dozen donuts with sprinkle covered lips on Instagram.

Dunkin' went a little bit of a different direction in they used a shotgun approach to choosing influencers. They chose many high-profile influencers, but the justification for that is that everyone loves donuts. Or most people love donuts. The choice to move forward with this approach even fits their ongoing brand story, "The world runs on Dunkin'."

Moxy Hotels of Marriot

Marriott Hotels is a well-known chain, but it has not been able to keep up with the younger generation. They are trying to compete with the generation that prefers Airbnb, doesn't spend much time in hotel rooms, and wants a cost-effective option with luxury experiences. Most hotel chains can't deliver that. To change up their role with Millennials, Marriott created a sub-brand where they could tell stories to younger audiences that focused on their needs exclusively.

Marriot created the brand "Moxy Hotels" and launched its own YouTube channel. They created a "Do Not Disturb" video series with

Taryn Southern, a well-known travel influencer. Southern would interview other influencers within a shipping container that was a recreation of a Moxy hotel room. The key takeaways from the Moxy Hotel run include:

- Southern fit the demographic and niche.
- Millennials proved with this campaign that they don't mind sponsored content regardless of the length of content.
- Long-term influencer relationships can be good for brands.

Practical Tips for Influencer Marketing with Storytelling

The important thing to plan is how to fit your influencer marketing within a scope that benefits your brand's storytelling. You already know that storyselling is substantially impactful, but how can you use one of the top marketing techniques side by side with storytelling?

Be Picky

When you search for the right influencer for your brand, you want to be extremely picky. This is not a spokesperson that has an obligation and a contract to speak about your company and present themselves in a certain way. Imagine if a family-friendly restaurant got together with a foodie-influencer only to realize afterward that the influencer they hired is a party person that posts about drinking, casual encounters, and risqué photos. That is not a good fit.

Find someone who:

- Knows your story
- Likes your brand
- Connects with your target audience
- Aligns with your brand's values and mission statement
- Understands your needs in an influencer campaign

A lot of pickiness can be clarified during discussions prior to agreeing to work together. You can outright state, we are family-friendly, so if your image does not fit that, then we're not a good fit for each other. That line "a good fit for each other" is really important to influencers, too. They do not want to compromise their brand or following for a one-time payment.

Let Go

The risk of hiring an influencer is that they are going to say what they want to say. They're going to tell the stories that they want to tell, and if you are too overbearing, they will drop out. They're not people pleasers who will jump through hoops to please a marketing representative. That is not to say that influencers are "divas," but you cannot give them a script and expect them to read it.

Influencers rely on a degree of honesty with their followers, and if they get caught (much like with the Fyre Festival) in a lie or bad marketing tool, then they will be in a world of trouble, and their job is at risk.

So, if you cannot let go or connect with an influencer that can take your brand's story and share one of their own to benefit your customers, then influencer marketing is not right for you.

Host Events

When you want some control over an influencer's interaction with your brand, you can sponsor an influencer event. Invite a small handful of influencers to come and experience your brand's products or services. By doing this, you allow them to become part of your story—very similar to what Moxy Hotels from Marriott accomplished. Influencer events give the brand and the influencer a stable platform for their interactions.

Ask for Meet and Greets

When you are drawing up your contract or agreement, you need to be very clear with your expectations, as you're essentially giving someone almost unlimited creative control, free products or services, and the time and energy of your marketing team. So be clear about what you want and ask for a meet and greet.

There is something about a meet and greets with influencers. They are a very special experience for their followers. Plus, if you are the brand that can deliver that experience, then you're the hero in the room. However, there is a bigger picture here, too—those guests, the ones that show up for the meet and greet, are now part of your brand's story as well. They're the ones who were part of a company experience, not just a service. They did not show up for a meal or a night in a hotel and get what they paid for; they received something that you delivered because of a unique approach to sharing your brand's story.

Chapter 9: Digital Storytelling

Digital storytelling is the act of communicating a story through computer-based tools and a digital medium. It could include blogging, digital essays, electronica memoirs, interactive storytelling, and much more. Through this chapter, you will see the different mediums as well as a variety of tools to use in digital storytelling. However, it is important to cover the foundation and how digital storytelling got started.

The Center for Digital Storytelling (CDS) was founded in 1994 in San Francisco only one year after the first-person narrative short film conference of the American Film Institute. What came out of this was an unexpected impact on storytelling. Before there was a focus on creating personal narratives and digital storytelling, storytelling was largely restricted to authors, screenwriters, motivational speakers, and entrepreneurs.

Digital storytelling made it possible for everyday people to share their stories in a medium that they preferred. Someone who had lived a fascinating life but had no writing skill could create a conversation-like video and post it to YouTube or create a podcast and share their story through that medium. Although digital storytelling still demands the same skill set in crafting and structuring a story appropriately, it offers a wide variety of tools and platforms.

Is It Storytelling, Digital Storytelling, or Something Else?

How can you determine if what you are doing is storytelling, digital storytelling, or something else? There are a few critical elements that appear in storytelling, as well as digital storytelling. However, the importance is more on the differences, and in recent years the lines have been blurred between digital storytelling and things like talk radio.

Here are the shared elements between storytelling and digital storytelling:

- Point of view
- Dramatic question or addressing specific issue or challenge
- Conflict and tension
- Emotional connection
- Unique voice or narrative tone
- Controlled pacing
- Structure of beginning, middle, and an end

Now the elements that only appear in digital storytelling, but not storytelling:

- Soundtrack
- Possible visual elements such as video, background images, or PowerPoint presentations
- Economy – purposeful withholding of specific information given in another format, such as through the soundtrack or visual elements

This book will cover the platform on its own a little later because the platform can determine if you are storytelling or presenting a digital story. But looking at the three differentiating elements of digital storytelling, you can see a clear pattern already. The economy of the story changes when you use a digital format. You can cut a lot of information you would deliver in traditional storytelling when you have supplemental material, such as a soundtrack, video, or background images. This is one of the reasons why digital storying took off. People could use supplemental elements, such as a soundtrack, videos, or images to make that emotional connection that they weren't able to make through wordsmithing alone.

So how about what is *not* digital storytelling? Well, there is talk radio. However, talk radio can include storytelling, and it can become digital storytelling when it is connected to the Internet or published through a podcast. Radio shows often have audio engineers that can create a soundtrack as the show is happening, which is one of the primary elements of digital storytelling. Also, radio hosts are extremely skilled at telling stories with a really strapped economic scope. While radio is waning, its replacement podcasts are gaining traction. As of March 2020, over 30 million households reported regularly listening to podcasts. Additionally, 55 percent of the U.S. population frequently listens to podcasts.

Podcasts and talk radio are not inherently digital storytelling. However, some shows use digital storytelling as the only purpose of that show's existence. For example, the podcast *Serial* took off because it was a digital storytelling delivery of a true-crime docuseries. Additionally, a long-time radio show, *The Phil Hendrie Show*, recently became a podcast and ended its time on traditional radio airwaves. Now, *The Phil Hendrie Show* uses storytelling; however, it is not explicitly digital storytelling. While this really seems like splitting hairs, you must understand the differences between digital storytelling and digitally accessible entertainment. To compare, *The Phil Hendrie Show* uses storytelling rather frequently. However, other shows, like *The John Tesh* Show or much of Christian radio, will occasionally pull from traditional storytelling and not use specific digital storytelling elements.

Let's Talk Platform

The platform used for storytelling can help you determine whether you are simply storytelling or using digital storytelling. As mentioned, podcasts and radio fall in a gray area. However, YouTube and blogging are explicitly digital storytelling. It has almost come to the point where if you're sharing a story online, you are using digital storytelling. Some common platforms include:

- YouTube
- Blogger
- Tumblr
- Reddit
- WordPress
- Webtoons
- Sequel
- Atavist
- Twine
- Medium
- iBook
- Shadow Puppet
- Apple Podcast
- Storify
- Shorthand

Clearly, this long list is indicative of how popular digital storytelling is nowadays. Now, choosing the right platform is a little tough, and many digital storytellers will use more than one to access a larger audience. For example, a writer using Medium to share their story may also publish that same blog to Tumblr and Blogger. This is one of the technical elements you have to consider as a digital storyteller.

Is one platform enough? And how can you ensure that you are using the right platforms for your stories?

When you are choosing your platform or platforms, consider the audience the platform brings in. Medium, for example, is a pay-to-access subscription-based platform. That means that if you want to access their content, you have to pay. For many digital storytellers, that is an ideal situation because it means that this platform delivers an interruption and ad-free platform. However, they have a limited base because of that required payment to access the content.

As a digital storyteller, you will likely use multiple platforms, and each one will have a bit of a learning curve. While this can be really intimidating, keep in mind that everyone has had to learn these tools within the last ten or so years. No one starts out having a high mastery of any platform, so be a little forgiving of yourself during the learning period.

Digital Storytelling Examples

Teachers use digital storytelling frequently as they attempt to accommodate various learning styles within one classroom. Additionally, pastors and preachers use digital storytelling to connect with their audience via PowerPoint slides and background music. So what digital storytelling examples can showcase the full effect of using a platform and various tools accordingly?

The podcast *Serial* was mentioned earlier, and it is worth citing again because it has a unique soundtrack and offers a documentary through the lens of storytelling. It's a podcast that grabbed attention far beyond the initial realm of podcast listeners, obtained numerous awards, and spurred at least two documentary films. *Serial* chronicles the murder of Hae Min Lee and the subsequent trial of her ex-boyfriend. Unlike other podcasts, it has a limited number of episodes, but not a necessarily conclusive ending.

Another outstanding example of digital storytelling is the Webtoons comic *SubZero*, which has over 9.3 million reads. It is a story about romance and sacrifice delivered in a comic-style format through an app called Webtoons. The creators are responsible for their own storytelling, artwork, and proper formatting. Basically, if you are an author on Webtoons, you're doing it all. This particular story blends many long-time tropes, such as the distressed hero and sworn enemy, with a modern twist through a visual medium.

Finally, an interactive online content example is Inequality. This is where you can explore the disparity of economic wealth between the top 10 percent of Americans and everyone else. In this content, you follow the "story" as the primary character with factual information, playful interaction, and an engaging storyline. It works with themes of political statements and economic insights that impact many Americans of all wealth classes.

How Can You Start a Digital Story?

Starting a digital story is much like starting a traditional story. You should create your first draft as though you are going through with traditional storytelling, even though you have the opportunity to be much more economical with your storytelling. It can help you make decisions about supplemental elements, such as a soundtrack, later.

1. Create your first draft as though you're storytelling traditionally.

2. Choose the platform(s) right for your story.

3. Identify what elements you need to build your story – audio, visual, interactive.

4. Learn the tools of the trade.

5. Create your supplemental or digital elements.

6. Combine all elements of the story.

7. Post to your platforms.

Do not set time limits on yourself for each of these steps. The quality of the story and the digital elements, including the video and soundtrack, are far more important than finishing your story quickly. Keep in mind that if you want to be a perpetual digital storyteller, the time you dedicate to learning the rules will help with every story you do after your first story. Also, remember to enjoy the process. It is exciting to get your work out there and have an audience read and interact with it, but it's just as important that you relish crafting it.

Best Practices for Digital Storytelling

As with most things in storytelling, there are a few best practices for making an effective digital story. These best practices are not set in stone rules, but they are things to consider before you start drafting. When you know these elements of writing, editing, and publication, you can have much more control over your story before deciding how to release it.

Make the Story Personal

People love personal stories. It is something about sharing a human experience and likely one that your audience has not experienced. Your personal story can immediately deliver something that readers crave across all platforms and entertainment types—why. Humans naturally question a series of events, and when you are presenting a personal story, you're saying, "This happened, and this is why." It is powerful and captivating, and it's the basis of a lot of fiction. Webtoon is a platform that holds fiction depicted as personal stories. The audience does not know if these stories are true or not, and in most cases, it doesn't matter.

Making the story personal does not mean that you are detailing a real-life event that happened to you. What it means is that you're inserting a piece of yourself and delivering a story that is something that many people can identify with.

Choose Your Platform and Publishing Method Strategically

When you are a digital storyteller, choosing your platform makes a huge impact on how successful your story is because of the access you have to the right audience. The best practice is with choosing your platform, and deciding how to publish your digital story, largely revolves around casting a wide net. Never limit yourself to a single platform. Additionally, make sure that one platform feeds into another, and that feeds into another.

For example, if you have chosen a podcast, it may seem like your platform options are very limited. However, you can publish to Spotify and Apple podcast. You can, and should, create episode notes that read like a blog, and post those to your website or Tumblr. In fact, you are not limited to publishing those blog-like episode notes to multiple platforms. Some platforms like Medium allow you to include an audio link so your audio can play alongside your episode notes.

Do not limit yourself. Make sure that you have enough options available to reach your audience.

Ensure That Your Narrative Has a "Feel"

Remember the saying, "It's not what you say; it's how you say it"? That is the foundation of giving your narrative a feel. When you are storytelling in front of an audience, public speaking, or using digital storytelling, you can give more life to the tone of your narrative. You can use music or voice inflection to make a point in your story more dramatic or more comedic than it would have been if someone were reading it off a blog post. Additionally, if you're posting to a blog, you have the opportunity to include funny memes or images of an incident to really showcase what happened in your story.

With traditional storytelling, word choice determines your narrative. But when it comes to digital storytelling, you have a marriage between word choice and your additional mediums. You learn how to give your narrative more of a feel as you explore digital storytelling tools. Again, this is one of those things that you learn through doing, and you will improve that skill over time. As a digital storyteller, the tools to help you build your narrative tone will continue to change and evolve. You have to change and evolve with the times as well.

Get Outside Your Comfort Zone

Throughout this chapter, it has been clear that digital storytelling requires any storyteller to step outside of their comfort zone. You are working with new mediums and platforms, and even if you're an experienced storyteller, this will probably be fairly new to you. In fact, the following is an example of a version of digital storytelling that evolved quickly, and both of the creators were unfamiliar with this particular medium.

The hit American adult animation series, *Rick and Morty*, is a raunchy science fiction animation series that did not start out as a project meant for TV. It was created by two friends, Justin Roiland and Dan Harmon, whom both loved storytelling. So, where did *Rick and Morty* actually start? *Rick and Morty* began as a parody of Doc Brown and Marty from *Back to the Future* that was posted to YouTube irregularly. There was no goal to take it to a huge network to become a successful show; Roiland and Harmon were simply telling outrageous sci-fi stories with an adult element based on two characters that they enjoyed from a film. Now, both these men had worked in the entertainment industry, so they were experienced storytellers. Harmon was a comedian and sitcom creator, who created and produced the show *Community*; Roiland was a voice actor, writer, and comedian. At the point when they started *Rick and Morty*, neither of them had experience animating stories. However, they learned, and the show has seen substantial success.

The key takeaway from this example is that you can explore new mediums with great success. Audiences of digital storytelling often understand that the creators wear many hats. They are often willing to wait much longer to continue a story and will accept lower quality visual or audio effects than they would expect from a professional studio.

Tools to Use in Digital Storytelling

There has been much discussion about digital storytelling tools and how to approach the multimedia elements of creating your story. Thankfully, there are a handful of excellent tools available to digital storytellers online, and most of them are free. When you are bringing together multiple computer-based tools, such as computer animation or voice casting, along with storytelling, things can get complicated very quickly. As a digital storyteller, it is important to have tools to follow your projects from beginning to completion.

Tools for monitoring your story's development:

- Project management tools - Asana or Monday
- Calendar - Set goals on your paper calendar, and keep track of when you complete milestones
- Organizational tools - Trello to keep all of your characters, digital medium information, and progress in check

Tools for creating:

- Animaker Class - Learn how to use a simple set of tools to make whiteboard animations, 2D animators, presentations, and more
- 30hands Learning - A user-friendly iOS app that allows you to narrate photos and create a story with strong visual elements
- Story Bird - Create short art
- Capzles - Create multimedia stories with videos, photos, blogs, and more
- Domo Animate - Develop animated stories with different backgrounds and characters
- ZimmerTwins - Explore all of your imaginative powers along with your storytelling skills by working with a web2.0 tool

Chapter 10: Immersive Storytelling

Immersive storytelling is a technique used to explore storytelling through new technologies to immerse the reader or audience fully. Long before immersion through Virtual Reality (VR) or Augmented Reality (AR), there were other ways that storytellers would create an immersive and truly unique experience. Of course, the key to storytelling is still about the story: the structure, content, and what the speaker has to say. That does not change when it comes to immersive storytelling. However, it requires much more of the creator. You are not simply a writer; you are possibly an animator, video editor, director, programmer, or more. The possibilities can vary so drastically that there is not a single path for an immersive storyteller.

In this chapter, you will find information on where and how to start an immersive story. Additionally, there are a handful of platforms currently helping immersive storytellers develop and share their stories. Finally, you'll have access to a broad spectrum of tools that can help with story development and working with different mediums. By the end of this chapter, you should have a full understanding of what it will take to create an immersive story, and a general understanding of the medium you'll use, and how to start building skills within those new mediums.

However, is immersive storytelling really something worth considering for storytelling development? Absolutely! If you are not sold on an immersive story yet, think about these quick stats about this growing segment of the storytelling world:

- Most consumers have already engaged in a 360-degree video experience (VR or AR).
- Twenty-two percent of consumers regularly use augmented reality apps, such as Pokémon Go!
- AOL's Video Industry Research Study estimates that VR consumption will increase by 31 percent in the near future.

Immersive Storytelling Through History

It seems as if immersive storytelling is exceptionally new, but it has been around nearly since storytelling has begun. While people look at oral tales and traditions as the beginning of storytelling, rituals and social practices were the beginning of immersive storytelling. These rituals allowed the people of the time to become more a part of their culture and devote themselves to perpetuating the stories and traditions of the society.

Then, throughout the middles ages, there was the implementation of storytelling stained glass in churches and other symbolic establishments. This practice continued throughout the Renaissance period as prolific artists rose and contributed their works to different mediums. Even though mosaic works had been present for some time when Michelangelo crafted the *Creation of Adam* on the Sistine Chapel's ceiling, it was considered to be a revolutionary work of art as it portrayed a story, which was new, and undeniably, immersive for the time.

After stained glass and mosaics graced religious centers to immerse the visitors in the traditional bible stories, immersive storytelling took another turn. By the late eighteenth century, a type of storytelling came into a play called Phantasmagoria. Phantasmagoria used a combination of smoke, mirrors, lanterns, sheer screen, early image projectors, and sound effects to give an audience experience. It is very similar to the Halloween experiences hosted at modern-day theme parks. The world-famous Universal Studios' Halloween Horror Nights and Knott's Berry Farm's Halloween Haunt use these practices with actors and intricate mazes for an immersive storytelling experience. Immersive storytelling, such as Phantasmagoria, is proof that you do not need intricate technology or programming skills to establish an extraordinary experience.

Then, in 1930, a toy would change the course of immersive storytelling. When the View-Master appeared, and children were looking into these small toys to see the African Savannah or China's Great Wall, it wasn't yet full storytelling, but it was the foundation for what would lead to VR headsets. The game changed again with the introduction of Choose Your Own Adventure books. These books allowed the reader to change the process and outcome of the story drastically. As they read, they would make decisions and jump to different pages to progress with their story.

Today, people use mobile devices, computers, and gaming consoles to experience stories through immersive interaction and engagement. Video games, such as *Detroit* or *Until Dawn*, offer an experience similar to that of the Choose Your Own Adventure books, while the Oculus Rift has devoted its console to immersive 360-degree experiences, where the user often cannot see or hear the "real" world while playing the game or watching the video. Games, videos, and even chatbots can now deliver one-of-a-kind immersive storytelling experiences.

Where to Start and Outlining Tips

Knowing where to start with any story is rough, but knowing how and where to start with an immersive story is exceptionally difficult. You must decide where and how the experience will begin. It is always best to outline the initial story that you have crafted and then escalate it to an immersive experience. You may have your ideal beginning, middle, and end, and then accompany the middle and end with a variety of possibilities through different mediums. But the point here is to start simple, as though you were crafting an ordinary story that you might share through a book, short video, presentation, or business meeting.

After you have your first line of the story, or possibly the only story if you are creating immersion through video experience rather than choice experience, you want to move forward with an outline. You might have created an outline initially for your story, but now you will need to create an outline for the immersive experience. The leading creators in immersive storytelling suggest that new creators begin with the tried and true scientific method. You might recall the scientific method from school, where you created a hypothesis, did research, tested, and found your conclusions as a true or false hypothesis. Very similarly, you need to establish your hypothesis (what you think should happen, the original storyline), research, develop, test, and eventually create a final product.

Using "hypothesis-driven design," you can build an immersive story. Although the process itself is not exhaustive, it is exhausting. Follow these steps only after you have the initial conceived story:

1. *Research* - Explore your mediums, understand if your story will have different endings or options for the audience, and research how different storylines and your medium may interact or disagree with each other.

2. *Plan* - Create a visual layout for what medium elements you need (programming for games/apps, visual development for videos and games, etc.).

3. *Sketch, Test, Review* - Working with a medium, especially a new one, is never easy. Take your time to sketch the possibilities, test them, and review for possible development or improvement.

4. *Build* – After working with your medium and story, you can start building the actual product. Be it a game, app, video, or Choose Your Own Adventure-style immersive story, you will hit a point where you need to start creating the vessel that will deliver your story.

5. *Test* – You'll have a repeated testing period. Think of this as editing for your medium, rather than just editing your story.

6. *Learn* – Make clear takeaways from your test and learn how to implement the changes needed for a successful final result.

7. *Build Again* – You may not have to start from scratch, but you will need to revisit your medium's or platform's core structure.

8. *Test Again* – Testing is critical because it's the only way you'll understand your audience's experience upon release. You need to continue this cycle of building and testing until you're happy with the product.

9. *Launch* – Whether it's posting your video for use with a VR device, a game, app, or other platforms, you need to make your immersive experience available to your audience! It's exciting and thrilling, but know that you're not done yet!

10. Update – Very few immersive stories go through a launch without having subsequent updates. Updates allow the storyteller to ensure that the audience's experience is exactly what they wanted. It also helps correct bugs in programming code, glitches in video, and issues with audio elements.

Tip 1: Focus on Steps 2 and 3

It is difficult to say if any of these steps are more important than the others. However, steps 2 and 3, where you plan and sketch out everything regarding your story, will help with every step that follows. Spending more time on these two steps will allow you to become more efficient in developing your story. So, what is the process of these two steps? When you look at their core functions, they are rather similar:

Map out all the possibilities.

Even if you are creating a Choose Your Own Adventure-type experience, you need to put some limitations in place. Then, if you're working with VR and one storyline, you need to structure your visuals to complement your story without overriding it. So map out all the options with these tactics:

- Mark out your most important points.
- Identify your plot's pivot points—where there are critical changes in direction.
- If you're posing questions to your audience, provide a limited selection of answers for them to choose from.
- Ensure that your plot has built-in navigational cues.

Tip 2: See the Trees and the Forest

While you will often hear people talk about the bird's-eye view, it is more important to switch between two primary perspectives. You want to know that you have a way to see the project as a whole, in terms of progress and content. That is the *forest* perspective.

Then, you also want to have the tree's perspective, the small chunks that you can manage and monitor closely. You might want to clearly segment out your story into very small or bite-sized chunks. That way, you can manage your medium and your story step by step. This *tree* perspective can help you create an end product because of how much attention you can dedicate to the details.

When you combine these, you can create something truly unique. Adopting both perspectives will ensure that you are a more conscientious storyteller as you take on the viewpoint of the audience more often than other storytellers who use more conventional mediums.

Tip 3: Know When to Call It Quits

This is not referring to quitting your story or project. Instead, it is about knowing when it's time to call it a day and declare your project finished. Many storytellers get into trouble while creating an immersive story because it's so easy to get caught in the build-test-build-test cycle. What happens is that the storyteller gets too immersed. They get stuck in the building, testing, and developing stages because it's a captivating process, and there is a dedication to perfection.

"Perfect is the enemy of good." – Voltaire

Voltaire's aphorism means that if you are so focused on creating something that is "perfect," you are defeating the purpose of good work. Obsessing over creating something perfect is trouble, and it can lead to a disastrous result. The quest to create something perfect can mean that the project never sees completion or slowly deteriorates due to overediting, self-criticism, and, ultimately, destructive behavior.

With immersive storytelling, you should consider having testers or beta-testers who can experience your story as an audience and point out possible improvements. You will eventually hit a point where there are fewer and fewer notes. When you reach a point where there are not any notes that are useful or fit with your story, it is probably time to wrap it up and call it a day.

Platforms for Immersive Storytelling

Every creator needs a platform. Often with storytelling, these are live event platforms. You can tell stories during conferences, through situations, such as TEDx Talks, podcasts, such as *RISK!* and even open mic nights at local bars and lounges. However, some people share stories through vlogs, commercials, and branding within their business. With the rise of influencer marketing, there has been a drastic jump in storytelling through platforms such as Instagram, YouTube, and advertisements. However, immersive storytelling can be a little tough to pin down because it seems as though there are limited options, but you will quickly become surprised as to how many options you have for platforms. What is even better is that many focus on storytellers' struggles of using mediums that they are not familiar with.

Perhaps the most popular platform right now is YouTube. On YouTube, you can create videos that users can use in VR headsets and other immersive mediums. It is something that you can deliver easily as millions of people post to YouTube. It's also a great platform because of how many people you can reach. Through YouTube's intricate algorithms with proper optimization, you can ensure that your creation gets in front of your ideal audience. It's not as complicated as you might think, and surprisingly many YouTube video tutorials explain how to optimize your post so that your content lands in front of the right people.

You are not restricted to flat video on YouTube, either. YouTube supports uploading and the playthrough of 180-degree and 360-degree spherical videos through browsers such as Chrome, Edge, Opera, and Firefox. Additionally, there is the YouTube VR app available through VR headsets and most mobile devices.

Hopscotch allows people of all ages to build games, art, stories, and more. It also has in-app tutorials to help its users learn how to develop immersive stories. Hopscotch markets themselves as "bite-sized coding," and has an app that you can use on your phone. It's the modern equivalent of what in the 1990s was called "homebrew" games, except these now look far better. Then there is the option of utilizing interactive chatbots to create a discussion for your user.

Dexter is technically a tool, although it is a platform for the building process of AI chatbots. You implement the answers and can create a story where the user is the main character, and your chatbot interacts with them directly. Many businesses and brands use Dexter to create a unique interactive experience for their customers through SMS messaging. With a simple text, a company can prompt a story or even prompt the user to share their story, and use AI technology to pull the appropriate response and build a conversation that pulses with storytelling elements. The result is a high-quality engagement that is both memorable and builds trust with the customer.

Conducttr has garnered a ton of attention as an immersive platform. It is a simulation platform that allows its user to develop scenario-based experiences. It's similar to *Second Life*, but instead of only playing through your own "story," you create experiences that others can enjoy and engage in as well.

Tools for Building Immersive Stories

Because of the easily accessible tools online, immersive storytelling is becoming easier to manage. Evaluate these tools as possible options for creating your story. Each can take some time to learn, but usually, it is well worth the effort. Once you build your familiarity and skill within that one tool, you can return to that tool and use it repeatedly in future stories or for your development and updates.

• Torch – A tool used for creating augmented reality. You use this tool within a mobile browser, and it's very simple. However, you're working with objects already within the app, meaning 3D models and characters that you drag and drop into place. However, you can use Adobe or Sketch to create and upload your own 3D models and characters.

• Blippbuilder – Construct AR without any knowledge of design skill or coding. You can turn marketing campaigns and immersive stories for sharing into reality quickly. Blippbuilder does approach their tool as a marketer's aid, where they can use predesigned packaging, ads, and print ads to build their AR experience.

• Twine – If you're not familiar with open-source software, it basically means that it's free, but only maintained by a community. Twine, fortunately, has a huge following as story creators of all varieties use it frequently. This tool allows you to depict non-linear and interactive stories visually. Basically, it uses a unique map construction to achieve that tree and forest view mentioned earlier.

• TextureWriter – The drag and drop solution to immersive fiction. When you're telling immersive fiction, you can simply drag and drop the story's blank bits into place. Of course, that means that you need to know and understand your story before you get building. But it's a great way to interact with the idea of multiple plotlines and possibilities working together. You can use visuals and other elements within this tool, too!

If you are not sure if you have the right ideas in mind, consider these popular examples of immersive storytelling. Netflix released a *Black Mirror* episode titled "Bandersnatch." It allowed viewers to make decisions that direct the story's narrative and ultimately resulted in five different endings. However, those endings could come about at very different parts of the movie. You could have a 30-minute experience and receive the same ending after having a 55-minute experience. Or you could have completely different experiences each time. This is an immersive story, somewhat in the style of Choose Your Own Adventure, and done with a tool similar to TextureWriter.

Another example is included in YouTube videos such as "Show It 2 Me," from one of YouTube's many successful immersive authors. They take a song or audio track and create a visual story with a 360-degree video experience that you can view while using a VR headset. One successful immersive author on YouTube, Symor, has over 723,000 subscribers.

With this combination of tools, platforms, and outlining tips, you should have everything you need to create an immersive story for your audience. It may seem rather new and scary, but only the technology is new, and that will continue to advance and adapt. You may create videos or engagement through AR, but this step in immersive storytelling is not the be-all and end-all. Immersive storytelling is growing, and with that, you can expect new platforms, better tools, and a larger audience of people seeking immersive storytelling.

Chapter 11: 7 Experts on Storytelling

Experts in any field are worth listening to. Why? Because these people, throughout the years, have developed their skills and abilities. They know their field intimately.

   The following seven experts have pushed their followers to become storytellers themselves and often speak on the craft of storytelling as much as they actually tell stories. They each use storytelling for different professional purposes, but their advice is largely universal and can impact your story even if it seems you have dramatically different reasons for storytelling.

   Gary Vaynerchuk

   "Storytelling is, by far, the most underrated skill in business." - Gary Vaynerchuk

   Vaynerchuk is an American-Belarusian entrepreneur, author, speaker, Internet personality, and the CEO and cofounder of VaynerMedia. VaynerMedia helps Fortune 500 companies as a digital agency. With a slightly different approach than other storytellers, Vaynerchuck has made a name for himself by applying the rules of storytelling differently.

He has laid out a consistent storytelling method, which is why so many people look to him for storytelling advice and insight. What he constantly delivers, which is not a requirement of storytelling but rather a personal way of introducing or beginning a story, is backstory. He begins his stories as early as possible, sometimes long before he or his immediate family existed. In one story, he explains a long-forgotten trade agreement where Jewish people were traded to the United States in exchange for wheat.

Was that vital to the story? No, it was, however, a layer of backstory that served a purpose in acknowledging that your ancestral roots do not restrict the abilities of generations now to become outstanding entrepreneurs, inventors, and more. Giving "unnecessary" backstory isn't the only fundamental of storytelling that Vaynerchuk warps. During the "falling action" of his stories, he almost always directly states the value or takeaway he wants the audience to experience.

"Show don't tell" is what drives many storytellers to quit, and Vaynerchuk certainly shows quite a bit, but he is telling it so directly that it's integral to his storytelling method. For example, in a talk on storytelling and engaging an audience, Vaynerchuk hits the climax of his story, and says blatantly, "Patience. If you're feeling any angst, it's because you don't love the process more than the results."

Through purposefully bending but not breaking the rules of storytelling, Vaynerchuck can tell a story and inform readers of the value they need to understand. He uses this in business to build leaders into great storytellers that can empower their companies, staff, and consumers.

Seth Godin

"People do not buy goods and services. They buy relations, stories, and magic." - Seth Godin

Seth Godin is recognized as the creator of the successful e-mail drip campaign—those e-mails you receive where one offers feeds into another, and if you put them all together, they might create a cohesive brand story. He is a well-known author and entrepreneur who is renowned for his insight and contributions to marketing, modern advertising, business ventures, and leadership.

Possibly his most well-known book, *All Marketers Are Liars*, has some of the best advice and insight into storytelling. He urges marketers to use a story to make promises to the consumer and then deliver on that promise through business practices.

Through other platforms, Godin pushes marketers and storytellers to be more authentic. However, he wants story creators to change the way they think about authenticity, and even argues in that same vein that the current belief of authenticity is a "crock." Godin says that whatever is in the storyteller's heart is authentic. If it is selfish, then it's selfish and authentic. But that does not mean some extent of selfishness isn't also generous. Marketers and storytellers always want to achieve something, and they can get that and give, too.

The takeaways here are to tell the story that is true to you, do it unapologetically, be transparent, and make a promise you can keep.

Peter Guber and Tony Robbins

"A story emotionalizes the information." - Peter Guber

"We are defined by the stories we tell ourselves." - Tony Robbins

Peter Guber is the CEO/chairman of Mandalay Entertainment and has many other accomplishments.

Tony Robbins is a professional mentor and speaker, and one of the most sought-after motivational speakers of our time.

Both these men use storytelling, and often together, to help people and businesses change the way they think and lead their lives. It is one of the most impactful methods of storytelling, and you can see it in action.

Peter Guber built a career as a storyteller by trade and craft while running major movie studios and handling other mediums. However, it was not until pretty far into his career that he realized stories are the vessel for transmitting the information. Afterward, he began using storytelling strategically in his daily life to push his colleagues and coworkers to realize what they already knew.

Guber has specific advice for storytellers, no matter the field:

- Only tell a purposeful story if you have a goal.
- Be interested, rather than be interesting.
- It's not a monologue; it's a dialogue.

"Being true to yourself involves showing and sharing emotions. The spirit that motivates most great storytellers is 'I want you to feel what I feel,' and the effective narrative is designed to make this happen. That's how the information is bound to the experience and rendered unforgettable." – Peter Guber

Tony Robbins works with people directly and in huge conferences. He places his emphasis on empathy. With a desire to help people, he shows people how one story can become another by changing the perspective and adding empathy. He tells storytellers that what brings them excitement is fear, and fear rules their lives. In telling a story and making choices, their personal story can be freedom or prison.

Robbins receives recognition for a particular quote that he uses often but stems back to Henry Ford. He uses this disruption to complement what most traditional storytelling shows: "If you do what you've always done, you'll get what you've always gotten." Ford's quote is a succinct way of summing up the traditional story spine: "Everything was the same, until one day..."

The takeaway from these two speakers is that a purposeful story is a dialogue, and a personal story can change by changing the perspective or lens. What one person sees as suffering, can be used in storytelling with a purpose to engage a dialogue and reveal that they are actually the underdog who came out on top.

Simon Sinek

"Stories are attempts to share our values and beliefs. Storytelling is worthwhile when it tells what we stand for." – Simon Sinek

Sinek, a leadership guru and professor at Columbia University, founded a corporate refocusing company named SinekPartners. He is well known for his use of the golden circle, and his novel on storytelling and development, *Start With Why*.

Throughout Sinek's extensive storytelling experience, he has repeatedly circled back to three key bits of advice:

1. *Change the perspective.* An effective speaker and storyteller is always a giver and approaches storytelling with a giving attitude. If you are throwing your logo or e-mail onto every PowerPoint slide or pushing a product, you're doing it wrong. Storytelling should never be about you.

2. *Don't start by building a rational argument with facts and figures.* Give the audience something to believe in. Then prove your point later.

3. *Capture people's attention without interrupting.* That is what a story is: attempting to capture someone's attention and change their beliefs or perspectives.

These three pieces of advice show storytellers that the story is critical, but they, as the teller, are not. It is not about your research, your product, or your speaking; it's about the audience. Give them an experience, a story to connect with, and something captivating enough to supplement their lives rather than interrupting them.

David JP Phillips

David JP Phillips, a professional speaker dedicated to the scientific study of storytelling, is no stranger to crafting stories. However, he offers a formulaic approach and even shows how most workplaces do wrong by their staff and customers.

In a TEDx Talk, Phillips dove into how most meetings, conversations, and other interactions spur a "devil's cocktail" of hormones. When there are cortisol and anxiety in your brain, it causes you to become irritable, less focused, have less enabled memory capabilities, and generally produce unhappiness. On the other side, the "angel's cocktail" spurs your brain to create dopamine, oxytocin, and other feel-good hormones like endorphins.

Phillips equates a good story to the only other shared human experience that produces this flood of good-feeling hormones: falling in love. Through a scientific lens, falling in love causes you to drown in feel-good hormones for about thirteen months, the honeymoon phase. It sends your neurotransmitters on vacation, and everything seems better. Your mind is more focused, you have more motivation, and you even have a better memory because of dopamine and oxytocin.

A story can recreate that sensation, and it does not have to be about love, but it does need to follow a certain pattern.

To deliver a feel-good, inspiring story that grabs attention, motivates people, and improves their memory, you have to prompt the brain for those responses. You need to rely on the science and dynamics of storytelling that makes people feel relaxed or engaged. To accomplish that you must:

1. *Understand that there is no "static" storyteller.* Essentially, there is no one way to tell a story, and that any story could, in theory, fit with any storyteller. Your story may be unique to you, but you're not the only one who can deliver it.

2. *Write down your stories, don't just tell them.* Everyone shares different types of stories with colleagues, friends, customers, and so on. As people do this, they change and adapt to the situation. However, when you write down your stories, you're able to create a more static version that you can tell repeatedly with increased authenticity. Also, write down your stories for you. Not every moment

is an opportunity to tell that story you want to share. So, by writing them down, you can reference back to them as needed.

3. *Index your stories, so you know what stories you have and when they fit into different situations.* When you index your stories, you can weave them together and build larger stories with a bigger impact and emotional delivery.

Kindra Hall

"You could be the story that someone's waiting to hear." - Kindra Hall

Kindra Hall is a speaker, author, and advisor. She works directly as the President of Steller Collective and urges storytellers to take decisive action based on tangible advice. She uses storytelling for strategic use in today's communication challenges. Her advice?

Kindra encourages people who are embarking on their storytelling journey to focus on what they can control within their stories. She informs aspiring storytellers that they should not remove details for the sake of time and avoid mistakes as they can derail the effect and purpose of the story.

Humor is another big topic that Kindra addresses. Humor is woven throughout culture and society, but jokes specifically make people laugh at or with someone. Humor, however, causes people to laugh at something within themselves. When she tells her story of how she got started in storytelling, she brings in the humor of sibling annoyance. Her brother's silent laughter from the back seat of a minivan was annoying because, well, "little brothers are always annoying," which caused her to laugh recalling the memory, which further caused the audience to laugh because they could identify with her. Even if they don't have a younger brother, they know and understand the annoyance of a smaller child. They are not laughing at her little brother, but the annoying experience.

Finally, Kindra pushes people to find stories that share a part of the human experience. She declares that stories about life, loss, love, enjoyment, novelty, excitement, or disappointment are something that everyone shares. These shared stories are the foundation for strong relationships. Now, Kindra doesn't just share her stories for the sake of it; she shares to help businesses and companies develop their relationships, both internally and externally.

From these experts, you should take their advice only in ways that you can apply to yourself. If you are not telling funny or humorous stories, then you don't need to worry about Kindra Hall's advice on humor. Additionally, if you're not trying to reframe or rewrite a personal story, you might not be too concerned with what Tony Robbins says. However, these people are all experts for a reason. They give advice that reflects their approach to successful storytelling and building trust and engagement with an audience.

When you are working on crafting your story, it is always worthwhile to see what works for the people who have reached extensive success. After all, as the saying goes, "see what the best do, and then do better." Always consider everything that could be an element in your storytelling, and the experts here reveal the major factors to keep in mind. Consider the science and technology involved in storytelling as well as the medium, content of your story, and your voice as a narrator.

Chapter 12: The Future of Storytelling

So, where is the future of storytelling taking you? Authenticity will always remain king. It does not matter if it is fiction, poetry, a personal story, or a marketing campaign. If you are not giving your audience some piece of your human experience, they won't buy-in, and you will lose their attention quickly. This challenge for storytellers is one of the few things that will probably remain the same over the coming years. Expect there to be many substantial changes in storytelling within the next decade or two.

What is in the future for other types of storytelling? Through the current market of content consumption, creation, and marketing, it is estimated that people will see these trends in the near future:

- Never-ending stories (this audience always wants more, and constantly)
- Immersive storytelling
- Social impact storytelling (docuseries' and documentaries are on the rise because they're addressing real issues)

- Pushing the audience to become the author, as seen in motivational speaking sessions with Tony Robbins and digital VR experiences. Sometimes it looks like "story listening" will become the future where the initial storyteller prompts the audience to explore their own stories and marks upon the world.

Immersive content will likely have a drastic increase in the audience as the tools become easier for people to use. The result is more creation of immersive stories and a boost in their following. As this type of storytelling gets another huge jump inactivity, it is evident that storytelling will likely take another shift. How can you give a unique experience to each audience member? Okay, that is maybe a faraway concept, but immersive story creators are certainly creating the illusion of the audience having much more power over the story than is currently possible.

When it specifically comes to marketing, ads either become shorter or longer. For example, when watching an ad on social media, the advertisement may go far beyond the twenty-second standard. Why are you seeing ads that last over a minute, or maybe stretching to two minutes? These unfold because companies are putting more emphasis on creating meaningful stories. It is the chance to connect with people that could have a lasting impact on the brand, so it's worth the risk of making a very long advertisement, even it defies the industry standard.

However, in that same breath, long-form content is losing traction. This content often comes from brands and entrepreneurs through vlogs and blogs. The days of the 3,000-word blog reigning as king are over. People watched YouTube videos and influencers to feel connected to them, but now that influencers and YouTubers are well-known as marketing tools; people aren't buying in. They know that someone talking about their favorite way to cook at home will only lead to a food-delivery service plug, and it is getting old. Now people want bite-sized chunks of storytelling to avoid getting sucked into hour-long videos that are simply sponsored content.

What has been seen in recent years through influencer marketing and social media is clearly not sustainable. YouTuber after YouTuber and Instagram influencer after influencer calls it quits because of how demanding it is to have a lifestyle that does not align with your personal values. While the audiences are growing tired of being fed modified versions of authentic storytelling, the content creators themselves cannot keep up. Throughout 2019, many high-profile influencers and professional personalities ended their channels or brands because they created an image that they could not perpetuate and ultimately resulted in producing inauthentic content and the loss of some viewership. If you can't create authentic content, don't stick around.

The mediums and platforms, however, are still useful. Social media has made it very possible to reach a huge audience with very little effort. You are not trying to pack hundreds of thousands of people into an arena or get everyone to church on Sunday. Additionally, marketers are not hoping that someone is tuned in to NBC during primetime. Instead, they use PPC advertising methods and rely on different platforms algorithms to strategically plant their story with individuals who would ideally fit within the audience they wrote the story or commercial for. Having your audience in mind has been an age-old tip for storytelling. Because of technology, it has become easier than ever to craft a story with a very specific audience in mind, and then rely on these platforms to get it in front of the right people with targeted marketing.

But what will inevitably happen is that you will have the few content creators that chime in and out with inauthentic stories. Then you'll have the influencers or marketers with lasting power that deliver authentic storytelling, which reaches their audience in a meaningful way while also documenting the current culture and resonating with people emotionally. Companies that use storytelling marketing practices will likely give more power to the storytellers so that the message's authenticity is not lost in the attempt to push sales and convert leads.

Finally, data-driven storytelling is becoming a huge element in people's daily lives. Because of the huge spike in misinformation and disinformation, people want to know if a personal story is true or something made up. Storytelling based on true events and provided in a public forum has spurred people to become armchair detectives not just involved in stories of murder and intrigue but also relationships and similar events. People now make it a personal responsibility to determine if social media famous couples are actually "together" or simply staging a relationship for the hype. Again, it goes back to authenticity, and when the audience cannot determine if something is authentic or not, they want proof in the form of hard facts.

People are questioning facts more and more. However, they are still very willing to accept fiction as a functional part of their lives. Basically, audiences are not going to stop engaging with stories just because they are not true. However, they certainly don't want to be fooled by a company or influencer into believing that something is true when it isn't. If an influencer says, "26 percent of men wear makeup," the viewership will likely lose trust if that storyteller doesn't give information on where that statistic came from and how the study was conducted. But if the influencer were to say, "I know many men that wear makeup," the audience would happily accept that it was a personal observation as part of the story. If you're going to give some type of data, ensure that it's accurate and from a trust-worthy source, or better yet a variety of sources that all confirmed the same findings.

So how can all of this impact your storytelling? As you write your first story and get ready to present it to your audience, you will have to review a few big concerns because of these upcoming changes or possible trends. Of course, authenticity is the biggest concern, and you must always remain authentic, which means being honest with yourself and your audience. Then, you might consider the greater array of mediums available to storytellers. In fact, getting into immersive storytelling now could give you many more years of experience over the others who will enter the market when it hits its stride.

You should also look at marketing and engagement. Most storytellers are marketers to some degree. Even if you are only telling the story for entertainment, you want the audience to stay engaged and commit their time to your story. Explore how you can implement many different tactics used by companies or marketers to ensure that your content is easy to find, enjoyable, and gives something meaningful to your audience. Keep in mind, though, that storytelling should be a fun and emotional experience. Try to avoid getting so wrapped up in the technical elements that you rob the joy from experience, and instead put your focus on telling the story that really means something to you.

Conclusion

Congratulations! You now have an in-depth understanding of how to compose and present a story to an audience. Whether it is public speaking or using storytelling to build your brand through social media, you can put these fundamental concepts to good use. Keep in mind that you can always reference back to the basics here and pull from the expert advice to further develop your storytelling skillset.

From here, you will need to find your story and determine what medium you'll use to deliver it to your audience.

Good luck!

Resources

https://www.youtube.com/watch?v=hZh4N1vHybU

https://www.archives.gov/files/press/exhibits/dream-speech.pdf

https://blog.globalwebindex.com/marketing/campaign-of-the-month-hinge/

https://thedatingapocalypse.com/

https://blog.globalwebindex.com/marketing/brand-purpose/

https://www.campaignlive.com/article/why-dating-app-went-out-of-home-search-better-connections/1447760

https://talesfortadpoles.ie/blogs/news/the-power-of-storytelling-and-how-it-affects-your-brain1

https://blog.hubspot.com/marketing/storytelling-quotes

https://courses.lumenlearning.com/wsu-sandbox/chapter/parts-of-the-brain-involved-with-memory/

https://www.youtube.com/watch?v=Y8wol2nGSpY

https://abancommercials.com/luvs/tv-commercial-aposbath-apos-ad-commercial/27283/

https://brilliantdigital.com.au/digital-storytelling-quotes/

https://www.hcommunications.biz/blog/16-statistics-that-make-the-case-for-more-visual-storytelling-in-law-firm-content-marketing

http://safetychick.com

https://learn.teachingchannel.com/blog/2017/04/21/10-tips-your-authentic-story

https://www.wordstream.com/blog/ws/2018/11/08/brand-story

https://quotes.pub/joan-silber-quotes

https://thewritepractice.com/freytags-pyramid/

https://www.litcharts.com/literary-devices-and-terms/rising-action

https://slideplayer.com/slide/8198773/

https://www.keithbooks.com/folktales.html

https://www.dltk-teach.com/rhymes/goldilocks_story.htm

https://ecclesloeteromeoandjuliet.weebly.com/plot.html

https://www.goodreads.com/quotes/tag/editing?page=2

https://www.britannica.com/biography/Anton-Chekhov

https://www.goodreads.com/quotes/tag/show-don-t-tell

https://self-publishingschool.com/show-dont-tell-writing/

https://www.well-storied.com/blog/write-stronger-characters

https://www.youtube.com/watch?v=JZPkCntVNSo

https://study.com/academy/lesson/little-red-riding-hood-characters.html

https://www.youtube.com/watch?v=6Bo3dpVb5jw

https://www.youtube.com/watch?v=0RuzE6Zmn8o

https://www.briantracy.com/blog/public-speaking/tips-to-wow-a-crowd/

https://www.gingerpublicspeaking.com/article/3-storytelling-secrets-for-public-speaking

https://hbr.org/2018/08/how-to-stop-saying-um-ah-and-you-know

https://www.echostories.com/7-storytelling-resources-clarify-brand-story/

http://www.todayifoundout.com/index.php/2014/09/happiest-place-earth-history-disney-world/

https://www.youtube.com/watch?v=BdZjV3z__VU

https://www.searchenginewatch.com/2019/12/20/how-storytelling-boosts-content-marketing/

https://www.youtube.com/watch?v=aCCvZCacv8Q

https://www.b12.io/resource-center/content-creation/100-effective-company-slogans-for-inspiration-2020.html

https://www.thedrum.com/news/2016/03/31/1948-de-beers-diamond-forever-campaign-invents-the-modern-day-engagement-ring

http://appropriateinc.com/

https://www.google.com/url?sa=t&rct=j&q=&esrc=s&source=web&cd=&ved=2ahUKEwiAsNSb08_pAhVAHjQIHY40CeYQFjACegQIDBAF&url=https%3A%2F%2Fwww.saasworthy.com%2Fblog%2Finfluencer-marketing-statistics-2019%2F&usg=AOvVaw0_CWsucOuVZWT6iaaALu0q

https://digitalmarketinginstitute.com/en-us/blog/20-influencer-marketing-statistics-that-will-surprise-you

https://shortyawards.com/9th/dunkin-donuts-nationaldonutday

https://digitalistortenetmeseles.hu/en/history/

https://digitalstorytelling.coe.uh.edu/page.cfm?id=27&cid=27&sublinkid=31

https://www.podcastinsights.com/podcast-statistics/

https://inspirationfeed.com/digital-storytelling-apps/

https://www.webtoons.com/en/romance/subzero/list?title_no=1468

https://class.animaker.com

http://30hands.com

https://storybird.com

http://zimmertwins.com/splash

https://thecmoshow.filteredmedia.com.au/immersive-storytelling-frontier-of-virtual-reality/

https://theconversation.com/a-brief-history-of-immersion-centuries-before-vr-94835

https://www.mosaicmarble.com/blog/sistine-chapel-creation-of-adam-michelangelo

https://support.google.com/youtube/answer/6178631?hl=en

https://www.gethopscotch.com

https://www.conducttr.com/our-story/

https://www.torch.app/tour-the-app

https://www.blippar.com/build-ar

https://twinery.org

https://www.youtube.com/channel/UCV8Qe8z3RDLiAV7E0WP7-Fg

https://www.youtube.com/watch?v=5Itd5MrDmZ0

https://www.goodreads.com/quotes/904186-if-you-always-do-what-you-ve-always-done-you-ll-always

https://quotefancy.com/quote/1415861/Simon-Sinek-Stories-are-attempts-to-share-our-values-and-beliefs-Storytelling-is

https://www.youtube.com/watch?v=6GlpqIFbEqw&t=190s

https://www.youtube.com/watch?v=6GlpqIFbEqw&t=190s

https://www.youtube.com/watch?v=j3bYSltiRzk

https://www.singlegrain.com/content-marketing-3/7-examples-of-storytelling-content-you-can-use-in-your-marketing-campaigns/

https://ducttapemarketing.com/5-visual-storytelling-trends-shaping-future-communication/

Here's another book by Chase Barlow
that you might be interested in

www.ingramcontent.com/pod-product-compliance
Lightning Source LLC
Chambersburg PA
CBHW070048230426
43661CB00005B/811